P9-CCX-091

3 1668 03727 2421

CEN   CHILDREN 567.9 DIXON
    2007
Dixon, Dougal
Dougal Dixon's dinosaurs

Central   04/21/2009

CENTRAL LIBRARY

DOUGAL DIXON'S
DINOSAURS

The author wishes to express his gratitude to Peter Dodson, Ph.D., whose valuable contributions made the book possible. Dr. Dodson, consultant on *Dougal Dixon's Dinosaurs*, is professor of anatomy at the School of Veterinary Medicine and professor of geology at the University of Pennsylvania in Philadelphia. He is also a research associate at the Academy of Natural Sciences in Philadelphia. He has discovered dinosaurs in western Canada, China, Madagascar, Egypt, and the United States. He is also coeditor of *The Dinosauria*, the definitive dinosaur book for scientists.

Copyright © 1993, 1998, 2007 by Highlights for Children, Inc.
This compilation copyright © 1993, 1998, 2007 by Boyds Mills Press, Inc.
All rights reserved.

Boyds Mills Press, Inc.
815 Church Street
Honesdale, Pennsylvania 18431
Printed in China

Library of Congress Cataloging-in-Publication Data

Dixon, Dougal.
  Dougal Dixon's dinosaurs / by Dougal Dixon. — 3rd ed.
      p. cm.
  Includes index.
  Summary: The life and times of dinosaurs, from their evolution to the present-day discovery of their fossils.
  ISBN 978-1-59078-470-9 (hardcover : alk. paper)
  1. Dinosaurs—Juvenile literature. 2. Paleontology—Juvenile literature. I. Title. II. Title: Dinosaurs.

  QE862.D5D539 2007
  567.9—dc22

                          2006037876

First edition, 1993
Second edition, 1998
Third edition, 2007
Book designed by Bender Richardson White

10 9 8 7 6 5 4 3 2 1

DOUGAL DIXON'S
DINOSAURS

Dougal Dixon • Third Edition

BOYDS MILLS PRESS
Honesdale, Pennsylvania

ABOUT THE THIRD EDITION

We had fun updating *Dougal Dixon's Dinosaurs*. First, we added twelve newly discovered dinosaurs! Since our last edition in 1998, scientists have unearthed ten to twenty new kinds of dinosaurs a year. The author and Dr. Peter Dodson, a leading paleontologist, chose twelve of the most fascinating and important new finds. In order of their appearance in the book, the new ones are:

Antetonitrus

Gargoyleosaurus

Brachytrachelopan

Guanlong

Caudipteryx

Ouranosaurus

Falcarius

Agustinia

Alvarezsaurus

Masiakasaurus

Magyarosaurus

Achelousaurus

Second, we added more feathers! The evidence for feathered dinosaurs has gone from tantalizing to solid as a fossil. We included newfound feathered dinosaurs, and we updated old favorites wherever new evidence called for some kind of fuzz, fluff, or fan.

Finally, on pages 135, 137, and 139, we show how a variety of factors can create different fossil formations, rich in clues about how dinosaurs lived and died.

The Age of Dinosaurs is a fascinating destination. We hope readers will enjoy this journey back in time.

The Publishers

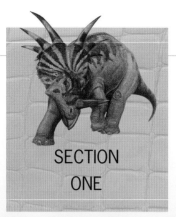

RISE OF THE

DINOSAURS

• EARTH • EVOLUTION • GEOLOGICAL TIME •

When we look at a dinosaur skeleton in a museum, a dinosaur model in a display, or a dinosaur picture in a book, we are at first amazed by the strangeness of the creature. We wonder that such an incredible beast could exist at all. Then, when we begin to read about dinosaurs, we begin to ask questions.

Where did the dinosaurs come from?

What kind of world did they live in?

How long did they exist?

These are all questions that scientists have been trying to answer for more than 160 years. Some answers come from the rocks in which dinosaur bones are found. The rocks can tell us about the landscapes of the past—for instance, sandstone typically formed from ancient deserts, limestone began as the shells of sea creatures, and shale and mudstone were once the beds of deep and wide muddy rivers.

DINOSAUR PARADE

Here they come! A parade of the animals that lived on Earth between the Late Triassic Period, about 228 million years ago, and the end of the Cretaceous Period, about 65 million years ago.

At the beginning, in the Triassic, there were all kinds of reptiles—digging reptiles, running reptiles, swimming reptiles, even flying reptiles. (There were also the first mammals. Those were small, shrewlike animals.) Among the reptiles were some crocodile-like animals, each with a long tail and strong hind legs. Scientists call these creatures the archosaurs. They became great in number when the other types of reptiles died out, and their descendants took up many kinds of lifestyles. One group of archosaurs began to walk about on their strong hind legs, holding their long tails out behind them for balance. These faster, more agile animals became the first dinosaurs.

As time went on, some dinosaurs developed

plant-eating habits. These creatures evolved bigger bodies to provide space for the plant-processing stomachs and for the long necks needed to reach around for food. They went on all fours because they could no longer balance on their hind legs. Other plant-eating dinosaurs evolved that could still run around on their hind legs; they had differently shaped hips.

The parade of dinosaurs continued in the Jurassic Period. This was the greatest time of the dinosaurs. The desert conditions of the Triassic gave way to moister climates in the Jurassic as shallow seas spread over the continents. All sorts of new dinosaurs evolved to live in the woodlands and forests of the new environments.

▼ In the parade of Triassic and Early Jurassic animals, we can see the first of the dinosaurs emerging. These included meat eaters such as *Staurikosaurus* and *Coelophysis*, long-necked plant eaters such as *Anchisaurus* and *Plateosaurus*, and two-footed plant eaters such as *Fabrosaurus* and *Heterodontosaurus*.

▼ Jurassic meat-eating dinosaurs included the small forms such as *Ornitholestes* and *Compsognathus*, and the big hunters such as *Dilophosaurus* and *Ceratosaurus*. Among the long-necked plant eaters were *Shunosaurus* and *Apatosaurus*. The two-footed plant eaters were represented by *Dryosaurus* and *Camptosaurus*. The armored plant eaters like *Stegosaurus* had also appeared.

PALEOZOIC ERA		MESOZOIC ERA			CENOZOIC ERA
	TRIASSIC PERIOD	JURASSIC PERIOD	CRETACEOUS PERIOD		
Millions of years ago 251	200	145	65	Today	

CROCODILIANS

BASAL ARCHOSAURS

PTEROSAURS

Sinosauropteryx
Protarchaeopteryx
Alvarezsaurus
Mononykus

?

BIRDS

RAPTORS

Eoraptor
Herrerasaurus

TYRANNOSAURS, ALLOSAURS (CARNOSAURS)

CERATOSAURS

PROSAUROPODS

SAUROPODS

DINOSAURS

Scelidosaurus
Scutellosaurus

ANKYLOSAURS

STEGOSAURS

Heterodontosaurus

HADROSAURS

IGUANODONTS

HYPSILOPHODONTS

PACHYCEPHALOSAURS

Lesothosaurus

PROTOCERATOPSIDS

CERATOPSIDS

SAURISCHIANS
(Dinosaurs with hip bones like those of lizards)

- Theropods
- Sauropods and Prosauropods

ORNITHISCHIANS
(Dinosaurs with hip bones like those of birds)

- Thyreophorans
- Ornithopods
- Marginocephalians

DINOSAUR ANCESTORS AND RELATIVES

All the dinosaur groups evolved from a group of the basal archosaurs of the Triassic Period. The archosaurs also gave rise to the crocodiles and the flying reptiles called pterosaurs. The dinosaurs gave rise to the birds.

DINOSAUR KEY

Nondinosaurs
1. *Rutiodon*
2. *Lystrosaurus*
3. *Cynognathus*
4. *Stagonolepis*
5. *Hyperodapedon*
6. *Kuehneosaurus*
7. *Erythosuchus*
8. *Ornithosuchus*
13. *Megazostrodon*
19. *Dimorphodon*
22. *Pterodactylus*
23. *Crusafontia*
26. *Rhamphorhynchus*
28. *Archaeopteryx*
(although many paleontologists regard *Archaeopteryx* and the other birds as dinosaurs)

Dinosaurs
9. *Anchisaurus*
10. *Coelophysis*
11. *Heterodontosaurus*
12. *Staurikosaurus*
14. *Plateosaurus*
15. *Fabrosaurus*
16. *Dilophosaurus*
17. *Scutellosaurus*
18. *Scelidosaurus*
20. *Compsognathus*
21. *Shunosaurus*
24. *Camptosaurus*
25. *Ornitholestes*
27. *Ceratosaurus*
29. *Stegosaurus*
30. *Apatosaurus*
31. *Dryosaurus*

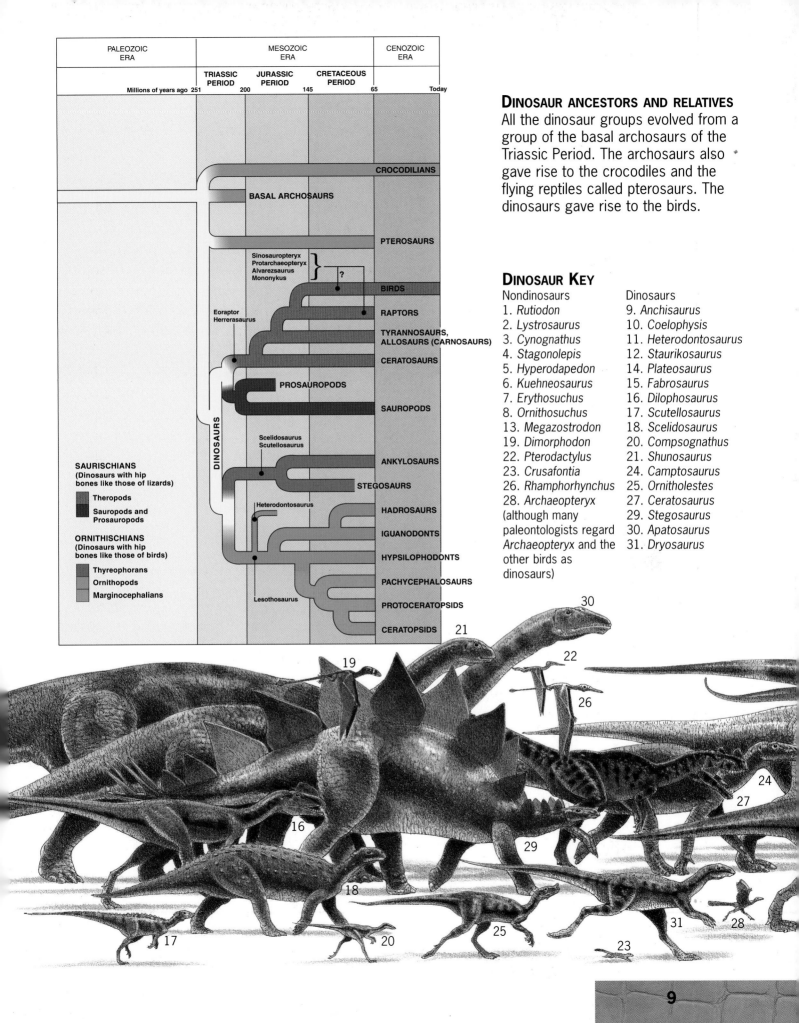

DINOSAURS MARCH PAST

By the Jurassic Period, the pattern of dinosaur development has become established, and the parade continues in this form until the very end of the Age of Dinosaurs.

The swift-moving little meat eaters were still around, but there were also huge, dragonlike meat eaters. These great killers evolved to feed upon the plant eaters that had also grown huge. The long-necked four-footed plant eaters were the largest land animals that ever lived. The two-footed plant eaters continued, too, and some of these developed into armored types—great heavy beasts that also had gone back to a four-footed way of life.

▼ Small Cretaceous meat-eating dinosaurs included *Deinonychus* and *Troodon*, and big ones were *Tyrannosaurus* and *Baryonyx*. Long-necked plant eaters such as *Saltasaurus* were less important in the northern hemisphere than other dinosaurs such as *Edmontosaurus*. Horned and armored types included *Triceratops* and *Euoplocephalus*.

The skies were dominated by the flying reptiles, the pterosaurs, but the true birds evolved at the end of the Jurassic Period. The small mammals still scuttled around, but were still insignificant compared with the dinosaurs.

By the Cretaceous Period, the parade had reached the peak of dinosaur development. Along with the small and big meat eaters, and

DINOSAUR KEY

Nondinosaurs	Dinosaurs
6. *Pterodaustro*	1. *Baryonyx*
7. *Pteranodon*	2. *Deinonychus*
14. *Zalambdalestes*	3. *Iguanodon*
	4. *Ouranosaurus*
	5. *Psittacosaurus*
	8. *Stygimoloch*
	9. *Edmontosaurus*
	10. *Saltasaurus*
	11. *Parasaurolophus*
	12. *Troodon*
	13. *Tyrannosaurus*
	15. *Triceratops*
	16. *Euoplocephalus*
	17. *Ornithomimus*
	18. *Stegoceras*

the long-necked and the two-footed plant eaters, new kinds of armored dinosaurs appeared, including bizarre horned types.

Up to this point the same types of dinosaurs had lived all over the world. Now different types appeared on different continents. A type of two-footed plant eater was the most widespread plant eater in North America, while the long-necked plant eaters continued to be most important in South America and the rest of the southern continents.

Then, at the end of the Cretaceous, just as they were becoming really spectacular, the dinosaurs suddenly vanished. The parade came to a halt. And along with the dinosaurs went the pterosaurs and other great reptiles of the time. The dinosaurs' descendants, the birds, survived and flourished, but it was the little mammals that really took over. So unimportant throughout the Age of Dinosaurs, the mammals survived the dinosaurs and went on to produce their own parade that brings us up to the present day.

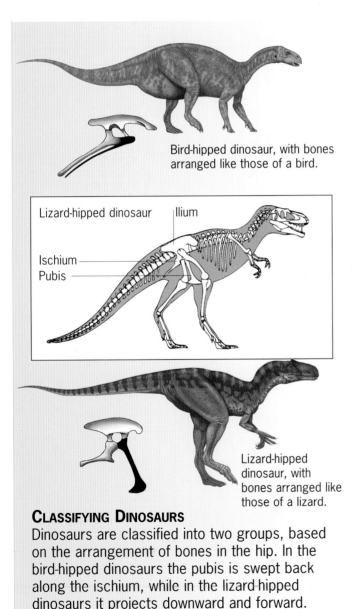

Bird-hipped dinosaur, with bones arranged like those of a bird.

Lizard-hipped dinosaur   Ilium

Ischium
Pubis

Lizard-hipped dinosaur, with bones arranged like those of a lizard.

Lizard—a typical reptile with a sprawling posture

Crocodile—with a semi-erect posture

Dinosaur—with a fully erect posture

Early reptile's sprawling legs   Dinosaur's vertical legs

CLASSIFYING DINOSAURS
Dinosaurs are classified into two groups, based on the arrangement of bones in the hip. In the bird-hipped dinosaurs the pubis is swept back along the ischium, while in the lizard-hipped dinosaurs it projects downward and forward.

DINOSAUR POSTURE
One feature shared by all dinosaurs is the erect posture. The legs are held vertically beneath the body, not sprawled out to the sides, and so the weight is carried at the top of the legs, not slung in between as in other reptiles.

EVOLUTION TIME SCALE

It has taken Earth a long time to get to where it is today—about 4.6 billion (4,600,000,000) years, in fact. At first Earth was a ball of cold dust. Then it started to solidify. There have probably been living things of some sort present on Earth as long as its surface has been solid and cool enough to support them.

The first steps toward life forms would have been molecules of matter that could reproduce, or make copies of themselves. Any change to these molecules that would have improved their chances of reproduction would then be carried on to the next molecules. Then the machinery of evolution would have been set in motion. Evolution is a process by which new kinds, or species, of living things develop from others.

These early forms of life left no remains, or fossils, and for about seven-eighths of Earth's history we have only the vaguest idea of what types of living things were around.

Then, about 540 million years ago, animals with hard shells evolved. Many of these creatures

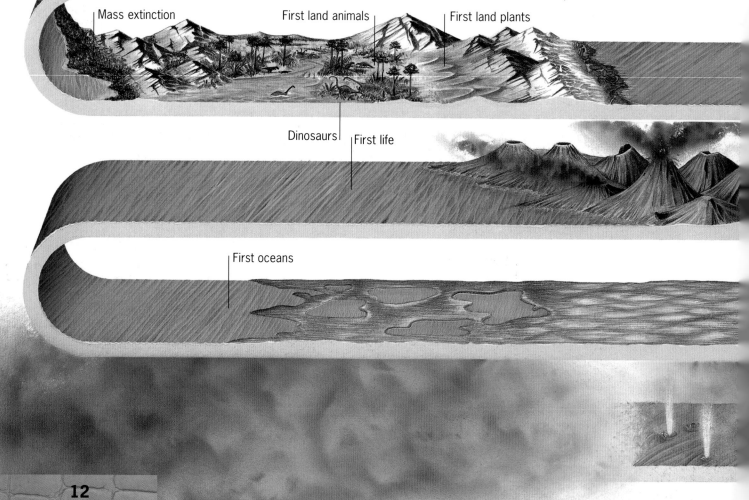

Ice age

Mass extinction   First land animals   First land plants

Dinosaurs   First life

First oceans

12

produced fossils. From that time we have a clearer picture of how life developed. At first all creatures lived in the sea. But about 420 million years ago, plants and animals began to live on the land. Some fish left the water and evolved into amphibians, of which present-day frogs and toads are examples. From these animals, the reptiles evolved. The period of time between 251 million and 65 million years ago is known as the Age of Reptiles. Within this period was the time of dinosaurs. When the big reptiles vanished, the Age of Mammals began, and this era has lasted to the present day.

▼ The evolution of, or changes to, the surface of Earth, from the time it started to cool until the present day. Each level of the folded band covers a little more than one billion years.

First hard-shelled animals

First traces of oxygen in atmosphere

Earth cooling

Precambrian (4,600,000,000 years ago)

GEOLOGICAL PERIODS

Geology is the study of Earth's rocks. Geological time, Earth's life span, is so long that scientists find it helpful to divide it up into sections called periods. Each period is marked by the kinds of animals that existed at that time and hence on the fossils that we find in the rocks that were laid down then. The dinosaurs lived in the Age of Reptiles—the Triassic, Jurassic, and Cretaceous periods. All dates are in millions of years ago (mya).

Holocene 0.01–0 mya
Modern times.

Pleistocene 1.8–0.01 mya
Ice-age mammals including early humans.

Pliocene 5.3–1.8 mya
Cool climates. Mammal life similar to present day.

Miocene 23–5.3 mya
Mountain ranges form. Many grass-eating, running mammals.

Oligocene 34–23 mya
Cool climate. Mammals start to look like modern types.

Eocene 56–34 mya
Forests. Mammals widespread.

Paleocene 65–56 mya
Forests. Many kinds of new mammals develop.

Cretaceous 145–65 mya
Forests, then shallow seas. Last of the dinosaurs.

Jurassic 200–145 mya
Shallow seas, dry lands, wooded islands. First birds.

Triassic 251–200 mya
Dry land with deserts. First dinosaurs and mammals.

Permian 299–251 mya
Mountains and deserts. Reptiles dominate the land.

Carboniferous 359–299 mya
Seas, swamps, then ice. First reptiles.

Devonian 416–359 mya
Mountains and lakes. Fish dominate. First amphibians.

Silurian 444–416 mya
Ice caps over seas, then open seas. First life on land.

Ordovician 488–444 mya
Dry land without plants, then seas. First fish.

Cambrian 542–488 mya
Widespread seas. First shelled animals.

Precambrian 4,600–542 mya
Shallow seas. Only simple life.

THE MOVING WORLD

359–251 MYA
In the Carboniferous and Permian periods, most of the continents of the time (gray areas) were joined together, and the rest were drifting toward this great landmass.

251–200 MYA
In the Triassic Period, when the dinosaurs first appeared, the continents were jammed together to form a super-continent called Pangaea.

200–145 MYA
During the Jurassic Period, Pangaea was still one single continent, but it was beginning to split. Shallow seas flooded over much of it.

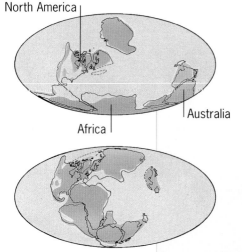

North America

Africa

Australia

We live, and the dinosaurs lived, in a world that is constantly changing.

The surface of the land is continually being worn away by the action of the rain, rivers, glaciers, wind, and all other kinds of natural processes. Over millions of years, mountains are worn down to rubble and sand, which are carried away by streams and rivers and dumped on plains and in oceans. There they form rocks, which can be folded up into new mountains and added to the continents.

Not only that, but the very structure of the continents is changing. And the continents are slowly moving about over the surface of Earth. Our planet consists of a number of layers—the core, the mantle, and the crust. The crust and a solid part of the mantle below it form giant plates on Earth's surface.

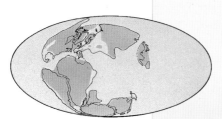

STRUCTURE OF EARTH
The mantle forms the largest portion of Earth. Movements in the mantle, in which molten rock material rises and spreads out and cool rock material sinks, are responsible for the movement of Earth's outer layers. The top layer is called the crust. It is Earth's skin.

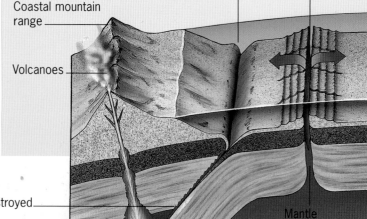

Ocean plate sliding beneath continental plate

Ocean ridge

Coastal mountain range

Volcanoes

Margin where plate is destroyed

Mantle material rising

Inner core—solid
Outer core—liquid
Mantle—liquid and solid
Crust—solid

145–65 MYA
In the Cretaceous Period, the end of the dinosaurs' time, Pangaea had mostly broken up into chunks that we would recognize as the modern continents.

65–1.8 MYA
During the Tertiary Period—from the Paleocene through the Pliocene, the early part of the Age of Mammals—the continents were drifting toward their present-day positions.

1.8 MYA–Present
During the Pleistocene, the continents stood close to their positions of today, in the Holocene. The continents are still drifting, and in times to come the world map will be different again.

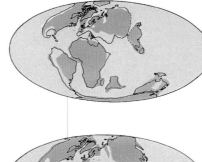

North America | Africa

Australia

PLATES OF THE CRUST
Each of the surface plates of Earth grows along an ocean ridge. Underwater volcanoes show it happening. One plate sliding beneath another forms an ocean trench, with volcanoes. At the edge of a continent this action forms mountains.

Earth's plates lie on a soft layer of mantle and so move around like leaves floating on water. At certain places molten rock forces its way to the surface to form new plate material. At other places old plate material melts and is swallowed up in the mantle. The continents are caught up in this movement and so the geography of the world constantly changes.

This is the mechanism that keeps the world's continents in motion. At the moment America is moving away from Europe, Australia is drifting northward, and Africa is pulling itself apart along a split called the Great Rift Valley. The movements take place at a few inches per year. The Atlantic Ocean is 30 feet wider now than it was when Columbus crossed it in 1492. Over millions of years, these movements create even bigger changes.

Continental crust | Movement of plates
Oceanic crust | Mountain range

Continent

Plate Material

Mantle

Continental plate collides with continental plate

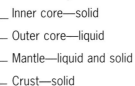

BEFORE DINOSAURS

The first part of the history of life on our planet is very unclear. All living things had soft bodies and left few fossils. Later, in the Cambrian Period, animals developed shells and other hard coverings—things we often find as fossils. From the Cambrian Period onward, the rocks are full of fossils and we can trace the evolution of life.

The first animals with backbones, or vertebrates, were fishes. These creatures evolved from wormlike animals that had a stiff rod supporting a long body. In the early fish, the stiff rod became divided into sections, making it flexible like a chain. Flaps evolved at each side of the body to allow swimming. And the brain

became encased in a box for protection. The basic fish shape, with a backbone, fins, gills, and skull, had evolved by Devonian times.

The first vertebrate to live on land was a kind of fish. It would have had a lung (so it could breathe air as we do) and paired muscular fins (so it could pull itself over land). It would have been able to live on land for only short periods. This may have allowed it to survive when ponds dried out or to hunt insects and spiders.

In Devonian times, the first amphibians evolved. They still had a head and tail like those of a fish. But they also had strong ribs to work the lungs, and proper legs with toes. Some

From Sea to Land

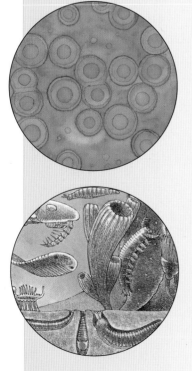

PRECAMBRIAN
4,600–542 MILLION YEARS AGO
The first living creatures resembled some modern blue-green bacteria. Mats of blue-green bacteria trap mud and build up lumps, which are called stromatolites. Fossil stromatolites are known from Precambrian rocks.

CAMBRIAN PERIOD
542–488 MILLION YEARS AGO
The first common fossils are found in Cambrian rocks. These are of spongelike and wormlike sea creatures, and of the first hard-shelled animals.

ORDOVICIAN PERIOD
488–444 MILLION YEARS AGO
The first fish evolved in the Ordovician Period, but the more common fossils are of lampshells, nautilus-like animals, trilobites, sealilies, snails, and clams.

SILURIAN PERIOD
444–416 MILLION YEARS AGO
Common fossils of the Silurian Period include trilobites and corals. Fossils of the first land-living creatures of this time are rare.

amphibians could live out of the water for long periods, yet they still had to return to the water to lay eggs.

In the Carboniferous Period, the first reptiles developed. Unlike an amphibian, the reptile lays an egg with a protective covering. Inside, a special membrane and fluid allow the growing and developing animal to breathe air. It does not need to live in water.

The Permian Period, which followed, was a time of deserts and ice caps. The amphibians adapted to the dry climate by evolving into armored land-living types. It was the reptiles, though, that did best in the drier conditions.

In the Triassic, the deserts continued. The big amphibians died out. The first mammals evolved from mammal-like reptiles. The archosaurs became the most important reptiles, evolving into several groups, including the dinosaurs.

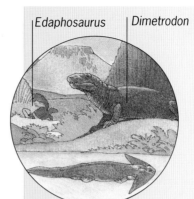

Edaphosaurus   Dimetrodon

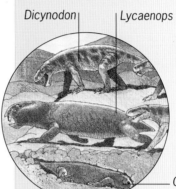

Dicynodon   Lycaenops

Cistecephalus

PERMIAN PERIOD
299–251 MILLION YEARS AGO
In the early Permian (left), amphibians flourished in the oases of the deserts, but more successful were reptiles like the herd-living *Edaphosaurus* and *Dimetrodon*, a hunter. The later Permian reptiles (below left) were somewhat similar to mammals in stance, appearance, and even tooth pattern. They included rabbitlike *Dicynodon*, wolflike *Lycaenops*, and molelike *Cistecephalus*.

EARLY AND MIDDLE TRIASSIC PERIOD
251–228 MILLION YEARS AGO
By the Triassic Period, reptiles had developed into many different types. The mammal-like reptiles included hippopotamus-like *Lystrosaurus*.

Lystrosaurus

DEVONIAN PERIOD
416–359 MILLION YEARS AGO
By Devonian times, land life was doing well, but in fresh waters and the sea, fish had become common. The Devonian Period is often called the Age of Fish.

Westlothiana

CARBONIFEROUS PERIOD
359–299 MILLION YEARS AGO
The Carboniferous forests were filled with amphibians and insects, and were home to the first reptiles that could lay eggs on dry land.

EARLY DINOSAUR PERIODS

In the Late Triassic Period, the first phase of the Age of Dinosaurs, the desert conditions still existed over much of our planet. All of the continents of the world were jammed together to make up one huge landmass called Pangaea. This supercontinent was so big that most of it was a long way from the moist winds of the sea. As a result, hot, dry conditions were common. The earlier Permian Period had been a time of mountains, formed over millions of years as all the separate continents crashed into one another. By the Late Triassic Period these mountains were mostly worn down to hills.

The animals living in this ancient landscape consisted of the last of the mammal-like reptiles such as two-tusked *Placerias*, archosaurs such as armored *Desmatosuchus*, and crocodile-like *Rutiodon*. There were also the earliest dinosaurs, for example *Coelophysis*.

As the continents moved, mountain ranges were still growing up along the edges of the continents. From the young Rocky Mountains, streams tumbled downward and spread rubble and sand over what is now Arizona. Along the routes of these rivers grew groups of conifer trees and cycadeoids, which were plants with swollen trunks that looked like the modern cycads. The small plants covering the ground of

LATE TRIASSIC—228 to 200 MILLION YEARS AGO

In an area that is now Arizona grew conifers, cycadeoids, ferns, and giant horsetails. The dinosaur *Coelophysis*, seen here among the trees, lived alongside crocodile-like and mammal-like reptiles.

1. Conifers
2. *Desmatosuchus*
3. *Rutiodon*
4. Ferns
5. *Placerias*
6. *Coelophysis*

these woodlands were mainly ferns. Reed-beds of horsetails lined the riverbanks.

How do we know all this? The remains of all these plants now lie in Petrified Forest National Park in Arizona. The logs of the conifer trees, turned to stone, now lie in the desert landscape where the overlying rock has been worn away by the weather.

In what is now South America, fast-running dinosaurs like *Staurikosaurus* evolved. In Europe lived *Plateosaurus*, the earliest known big dinosaur. In the early part of the Jurassic Period, the supercontinent Pangaea was still intact. It would not be long, though, before it would begin to split apart. Splits in the land began to form along the line that would tear North America away from Africa.

Shallow seas began to spread across the surface of Pangaea. These waters brought much moister climates far inland on the continent, and forests flourished where once there had been deserts. The seas flooded the low land between North America and Africa.

At that time, much of the continent of Europe, including Britain, consisted of low islands in a shallow sea. Giant sea reptiles, such as sleek dolphinlike *Ichthyosaurus* and the long-necked *Plesiosaurus*, chased fish and the coil-shelled ammonites in the warm, shallow waters. The islands would have been covered by a plant life looking like that of the Triassic Period. The early armored dinosaur *Scelidosaurus* lived here and had to guard itself against big meat eaters, and pterosaurs circled in the sky overhead.

At the other end of Pangaea, where South Africa now lies, there were plant-eating dinosaurs such as *Heterodontosaurus* and *Massospondylus*, and meat eaters such as *Syntarsus*.

EARLY AND MIDDLE JURASSIC—200 to 161 MILLION YEARS AGO

In what is now southern England, *Plesiosaurus* hauls itself onto the beach beside a dead *Ichthyosaurus*. The meat-eating dinosaur *Sarcosaurus* and the armored plant eater *Scelidosaurus* are nearby. *Dimorphodon* fly overhead.

1. Sarcosaurus
2. Dimorphodon
3. Plesiosaurus
4. Scelidosaurus
5. Ichthyosaurus

LATE JURASSIC PERIOD

• 161 to 145 MILLION YEARS AGO •

Apatosaurus

Brachiosaurus

Ceratosaurus

Mesadactylus

As the Middle Jurassic Period gave way to the
Late Jurassic, the supercontinent Pangaea began
slowly to be pulled apart. The shallow seas
continued to spread over the low-lying areas.
One particular sea, now called the Sundance Sea,
spread southward over the continent of North
America. It cut off the new mountain range to
the west from the main part of the continent to
the east. Sand and pebbles spread out into the
sea from the foot of the mountains and formed
a broad river plain. In spite of the nearby sea,
this plain was quite dry.

Plants grew in large numbers only along the
courses of the many streams. The rocks formed
here consist of sandstones, mudstones, and
siltstones in a great sequence of layers called the
Morrison Formation. Parts of the edges of the

Comodactylus

Allosaurus

▼ Plant-eating dinosaurs, meat-eating dinosaurs, and pterosaurs lived in and around a coniferous forest on a dry plain in Colorado.

layers can be seen in Montana, Wyoming, Utah, Colorado, and New Mexico.

The Morrison Formation holds such a wealth of dinosaur remains that it was the site of great dinosaur fossil hunts in the years between 1877 and the 1930s. The fossils discovered allow us to imagine the open plain, with forests of conifers and ferns along the waterways, inhabited by big plant-eating dinosaurs such as *Apatosaurus* and *Brachiosaurus* and armored dinosaurs such as *Stegosaurus*. These were hunted and killed by meat eaters like *Ceratosaurus* and *Allosaurus*. Smaller meat eaters and pterosaurs were there, too.

Stegosaurus

Ornitholestes

EARLY CRETACEOUS PERIOD

• 145 to 100 MILLION YEARS AGO •

In Early Cretaceous times the split-up of Pangaea was well underway. An ocean had opened up between North America and Africa, although North America and Europe were still joined in the north. Africa and South America were still one landmass, but Antarctica and India had broken away as islands. The shallow seas covering northern Europe had gone. A large marshy area, the Wealden, was left over what is now southern England, northern France, and Germany.

Iguanodon

Hylaeosaurus

Herds of *Iguanodon* and of *Hypsilophodon* move through the rich vegetation of what is now southeast England.

Istiodactylus

Baryonyx

Hypsilophodon

The dinosaurs that lived in the Wealden swamps included *Iguanodon*. It seems to have lived in herds, feeding on horsetail plants. We sometimes find *Iguanodon* footprints in the mudstone along with skin marks showing where these dinosaurs wallowed in the mud. Living in the swamps also were swift-footed *Hypsilophodon*, armored *Polacanthus*, and meat-eating or fish-eating *Baryonyx*. Big pterosaurs, such as *Istiodactylus*, flew overhead, and early mammals scampered in the undergrowth.

The muds and clays laid down in the Wealden swamps are known as the Wealden and Wessex formations. They contain fossils of conifer trees, ferns, tree ferns, ginkgoes, and early flowering plants as well as the animals of the time. Mud cracks and rain pits in the mudstones show where the shallow waters dried out from time to time.

23

LATE CRETACEOUS PERIOD

• 100 to 65 MILLION YEARS AGO •

By the end of the Age of Dinosaurs, Pangaea had ceased to exist; the supercontinent had completely broken up. North America was separate from South America and from Europe, and Africa had broken away from South America. However, Antarctica and Australia were still joined, and western North America was connected to northeastern Asia. Many places were covered by shallow seas. A broad shallow sea, the Niobrara Sea, cut North America completely in two from north to south.

▼ Heavily wooded landscape in what is now Montana. Herds of *Edmontosaurus* move across country, keeping well clear of *Tyrannosaurus*. Modern-looking birds fly overhead.

Edmontosaurus

Ankylosaurus

Triceratops

Thescelosaurus

Tyrannosaurus

Plant life was changing everywhere. The huge
forests of conifer trees and ferns were being
replaced by modern-looking forests of oak and
willow. Flowering plants formed the undergrowth. Palm trees grew in the warmer areas.
The region that today is Wyoming had such a
     forest, browsed by herds of two-footed
       plant eaters such as huge *Edmontosaurus*,
      horned dinosaurs such as *Triceratops*, and
    armored giants such as *Ankylosaurus*. These
   were all preyed upon by the great meat eater
Tyrannosaurus. These dinosaurs' remains have been
found in the rock layers of the Lance Formation.

THE RISE OF MAMMALS

The dinosaurs and many other creatures died out suddenly about 65 million years ago, a time that marks the end of the Cretaceous Period. We do not know why this happened. Possibly the moving continents changed the climates too much: the weather became too hot or too cold. Maybe diseases spread through the whole dinosaur kingdom. Or perhaps these animals could not cope with the changing plant life. Another possibility is that there was some kind of great disaster. Perhaps Earth was struck by a giant meteorite. Whatever occurred, the dinosaurs all perished, along with the other great reptiles of the time.

After all the big reptiles were wiped out, the little mammals that had played such a minor part for the previous 160 million years suddenly became important.

The pterosaurs, the flying reptiles, were replaced by winged mammals, the bats. The ichthyosaurs were eventually replaced by huge swimming mammals, the whales. The different types of dinosaurs—the meat eaters and the plant eaters big and small—were replaced by all kinds of meat- and plant-eating mammals. These spread from tropical forests, through deserts, to the polar wilderness. The birds, too, spread out and became much more important than they were before.

At first most mammals were forest-living types, but soon the forests gave way to grassy plains. Plains-living mammals later evolved, with long running legs and strong grass-eating teeth. These were the ancestors of the horses and the antelopes. It was the Age of Mammals, in which we are living now.

PALEOCENE TIMES 65 to 56 MILLION YEARS AGO
The Paleocene forests were home to tree-living mammals such as climbing *Plesiadapis* and *Chriacus*, and gliding *Planetetherium*.

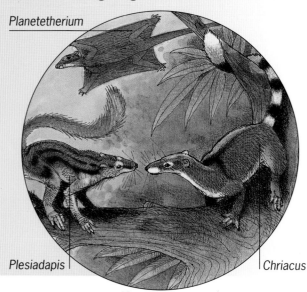

Planetetherium

Plesiadapis | *Chriacus*

EOCENE TIMES 56 to 34 MILLION YEARS AGO
In the Eocene forests lived huge rhinoceros-like *Uintatherium*, the little rhinoceros *Hyrachyus*, and the tiny earliest horse *Hyracotherium*.

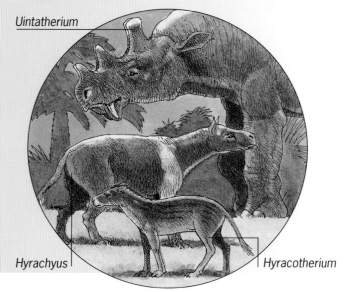

Uintatherium

Hyrachyus | *Hyracotherium*

THE AGE OF HUMANS

The dinosaurs dominated Earth for long ages. Today human beings do. All the known history of human beings is measured in thousands of years. The emergence of human beings—unique, self-conscious creatures—is a mystery. Scientists are tracking down physical clues like the similarity of other hominids (shown here) and man. There is much still to be learned. You may help learn it.

OLIGOCENE TIMES 34 to 23 MILLION YEARS AGO

The open landscapes of the Oligocene had big plant eaters, such as *Brontotherium* and *Archaeotherium*, and meat-eating *Hyaenodon* and *Hoplophoneus*.

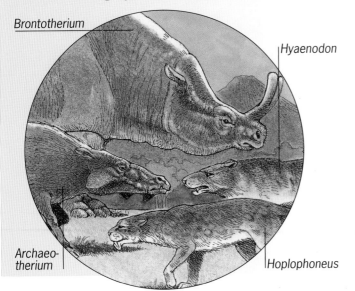

Brontotherium

Hyaenodon

Archaeo-
therium

Hoplophoneus

MIOCENE TIMES 23 to 5 MILLION YEARS AGO

The Miocene grasslands had the horse *Pliohippus*, gazellelike *Synthetoceras*, the camel *Megatylopus*, the rodent *Epigaulus*, and the elephant *Amebelodon*.

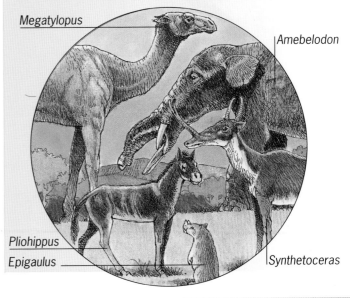

Megatylopus

Amebelodon

Pliohippus

Epigaulus

Synthetoceras

MEET THE DINOSAURS

• PANORAMAS • FACT BOXES • BEHAVIOR •

"Dinosaurs!" Mention the word and what do we think about? Five-ton meat eaters charging through dark forests, their huge claws ready to grab and kill any animal. Gigantic mountains of living tissue, lumbering slowly across the swamp, each with a tiny head on a long neck reaching for the leaves of tree ferns. Reptilian tanks, coated with armor, bristling with spikes and horns.

What a spectacle! And indeed all these kinds of creatures did exist during the Age of Dinosaurs. However, along with these there lived smaller dinosaurs—little crow-size beasts that scuttled about in the undergrowth at the feet of the giants. There were also medium-size dinosaurs, as big as pigs and sheep. They were all adapted to exist in particular ways in the landscapes of the times.

Their remains can tell us about what the world was like in past times—how the climates have changed, how the continents have moved, the distribution of land and sea, and so on. And as we try to build a picture of what dinosaurs looked like and how they all lived, we realize some of the wonders of our own world. During the 160 million years of the Age of Dinosaurs, the animal life was as varied and exciting as the animal life of today.

COELOPHYSIS

• THEROPOD • SMALL HUNTER •

Like a pack of wolves, the small group of agile creatures patters along the dry streambed. Each hunter carries its big head low, its keen eyes looking ahead for food. The animals' slim bodies are each balanced on long birdlike hind legs by a stiff tail. They hold their strong-clawed hands folded close to the chest.

Coelophysis was one of the earliest hunting dinosaurs. Somewhere along this stream course lay their prey—one of the big hippopotamus-like plant-eating reptiles that died out in the Late Triassic Period as the dinosaurs took over.

We know that Coelophysis moved about in packs because a mass of their skeletons was found in a quarry in New Mexico. A whole pack must have died together. Maybe they gathered around a water hole in a desert oasis until it dried up completely and they died of thirst. It has long been believed that Coelophysis ate their young in desperation during droughts. Bones of the youngsters were found in the stomachs of the adults in this mass grave. However, more recent research suggests that these bones were of small crocodile-like animals and not of Coelophysis young. Perhaps Coelophysis was not a cannibal after all.

In Connecticut, sandstone from the Early Jurassic Period is full of the three-toed footprints of Coelophysis or of some similar animal. Before anyone knew anything about dinosaurs, people thought these footprints had been made by birds of some kind.

30

COELOPHYSIS
SEE-loh-FY-sis

Length: Up to 9 feet (2.7 meters)
Height: 22 inches (0.5 meters) at the hips
Weight: 40 pounds (18 kilograms)
Food: Small animals and possibly large plant eaters
Range: New Mexico; very similar animals, but from Early Jurassic, in Arizona and Connecticut, and in Zimbabwe

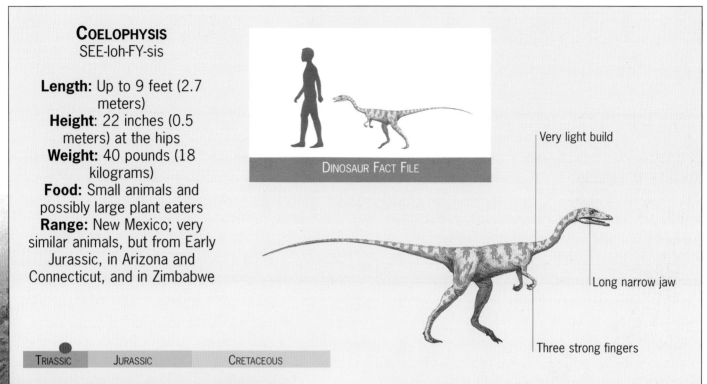

DINOSAUR FACT FILE

Very light build

Long narrow jaw

Three strong fingers

TRIASSIC	JURASSIC	CRETACEOUS

◀ The *Coelophysis* pack slinks along the dry streambed as the startled flying reptile *Icarosaurus* glides away. *Coelophysis* had teeth like carving knives. Its narrow flexible snout allowed it to grab small active prey.

▲ Modern wolves hunt their prey in packs, probably as *Coelophysis* did. A large pack can bring down prey bigger than any single wolf could. Working alone, each wolf has to be content with catching small animals to eat.

PLATEOSAURUS

• PROSAUROPOD • HIGH BROWSER •

Imagine the largest land animals of today—elephants, giraffes, rhinoceroses, buffalos. What one thing do they all have in common? The answer is that they all eat plants. Modern meat eaters, such as lions, wolves, and foxes, are all much smaller. One major reason for this is that vast amounts of plant material must be digested to gain enough nutrients to keep a creature alive and healthy. So a plant eater's guts—its stomach and intestines—must be much larger than a meat eater's to do the work.

It was the same in the dinosaur world. The first dinosaurs, in Late Triassic times, were small, fast-moving meat eaters, running about on their hind legs. Then the plant-eating dinosaurs evolved. Their big intestines meant that they had a long body and could not balance on their hind legs anymore. They developed strong forelimbs and began to move about on all fours.

The early plant-eating dinosaurs could still rear up on their hind legs for short periods, and this was a good thing for them. There were other plant-eating reptiles around, but they were like lizards and could eat only the ferns and horsetail plants growing near the ground. The first plant-eating dinosaurs were the only animals that could reach up and eat the leaves and conifer needles from the tops of the trees. They developed long necks as well, and this helped them to reach up still farther.

Living in large groups

Plateosaurus was typical of these early plant-eating dinosaurs. There must have been many of them, as several skeletons of *Plateosaurus* have been found together in one Late Triassic deposit in Germany. Some scientists think that this is because the animal lived and moved about in herds, but others are not so sure. Maybe dead *Plateosaurus* from a wide area were washed into a hollow in the ground when the desert streams flooded. The oases, or water holes, of the desert landscape probably had enough trees growing around them to support many thousands of these dinosaurs.

▼ *Plateosaurus* feeds among tree ferns on a hot, dusty Late Triassic plain. The arms of *Plateosaurus* were strong to support the front part of the animal on the ground. It could move its hands about freely. It used its thumb claws to pull down vegetation or to fight off enemies.

PLATEOSAURUS
PLAT-ee-o-SAW-rus

Length: 20–26 feet (6–8 meters)
Height: 6 feet (1.8 meters) at the hips when on all fours, 12 feet (3.7 meters) at the head when rearing up
Weight: 1,500 pounds (680 kilograms)
Food: Plants, probably from treetops
Range: Germany, with related animals in Argentina, South Africa, and China

Massive body | Long neck
Long hind legs
Short front legs
Small head
Five fingers and big claw on thumb

DINOSAUR FACT FILE

| TRIASSIC | JURASSIC | CRETACEOUS |

ANTETONITRUS

• SAUROPOD • HIGH BROWSER •

The earliest of the big, long-necked plant-eating dinosaurs, such as *Plateosaurus*, belonged to a group called the prosauropods. They were mostly small to medium-size animals and could go on all fours or raise themselves onto their hind legs to feed from trees. Their front feet had claws that were ideal for ripping down leaves.

The later group of big plant eaters are called the sauropods, and they developed from the prosauropod group in Late Triassic times. The way of telling whether an animal is an advanced prosauropod or a primitive sauropod is from the shape of the leg bone and the arrangement of bones in the hand. Since sauropods spent all of their time on all fours, they had straighter thighbones and did not have the big claws for pulling down vegetation.

Antetonitrus was the earliest of the sauropods. Its remains had actually been found in 1981. But its discoverers thought it was a prosauropod, and nobody took a close look at the fossils for another twenty years. The fossils sat on a shelf in the storeroom of a university. When scientists finally re-examined the fossils, they found that the bones were actually the remains of the earliest-known sauropod—15 million years older than any other previously found.

Antetonitrus was not nearly so big as the giants that were discovered later, but it was too big to walk on its hind legs. It still had a big claw on the forefoot, which showed that it was closely related to the ancestral prosauropods. It would have roamed the dry South African landscape in herds, along with the prosauropods of that time.

▶ "Before the thunder," that is what *Antetonitrus* means. And indeed it had the looks and habits of the bigger sauropods, the so-called "thunder lizards," that were to come. However, although it was bigger than any land animal from the present day, *Antetonitrus* was still much smaller than its descendants. It was even smaller than the biggest of the more primitive prosauropods that lived at the same time and area.

ANTETONITRUS
an-TEE-toh-NIGHT-rus

Length: 26–33 feet (8–10 meters),
based on an incomplete skeleton
Height: 6½ feet (2 meters)
Weight: 2 tons (1,800 kilograms)
Food: Plants
Range: South Africa

DINOSAUR FACT FILE

Straight thighbone

Fairly long hind toes

Claw on thumb

Lightweight hand

TRIASSIC   JURASSIC   CRETACEOUS

DILOPHOSAURUS

• THEROPOD • LITHE HUNTER •

The big plant-eating dinosaurs such as *Plateosaurus* and *Antetonitrus* evolved at the end of the Triassic Period. Big meat eaters evolved as well, and by the beginning of the Jurassic, there were many different types. *Dilophosaurus* was one of these. Whenever there is a new type of food available, something will evolve to eat it. A big plant-eating animal has lots of flesh, so big meat-eating animals evolve to hunt them. *Dilophosaurus* was one of the first big meat-eating dinosaurs, yet it looked like one of the small meat eaters, with a slim and athletic body. Its jaws were armed with long sharp teeth that it used for tearing up chunks of meat—possibly the bodies of all kinds of *Plateosaurus*-like dinosaurs.

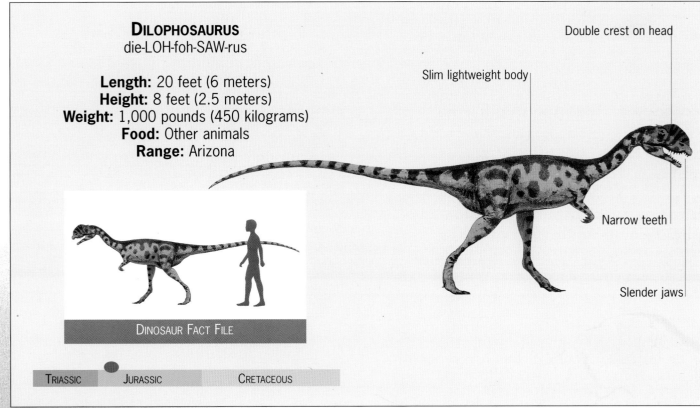

DILOPHOSAURUS
die-LOH-foh-SAW-rus

Length: 20 feet (6 meters)
Height: 8 feet (2.5 meters)
Weight: 1,000 pounds (450 kilograms)
Food: Other animals
Range: Arizona

Double crest on head

Slim lightweight body

Narrow teeth

Slender jaws

DINOSAUR FACT FILE

TRIASSIC	JURASSIC	CRETACEOUS

A name meaning "two-ridged reptile"

The front of the snout of this dinosaur was very narrow and flexible. Maybe *Dilophosaurus* hunted small prey, too, pulling out lizards and small mammals from the undergrowth and crannies in rocks.

Its skull is different from that of the later big meat eaters. Not only did *Dilophosaurus* have the bone joints that allowed it to wrinkle its nose, but it also had a pair of bony crests along the top of its head—hence its name. However, as in most dinosaurs, the skull is the most fragile part of the skeleton. It was missing from the first skeleton of *Dilophosaurus* that was found. The scientists who found the skeleton did not realize just what a strange animal they had discovered.

◄ Prowling by the coniferous forests of Early Jurassic Arizona, crested *Dilophosaurus* surprises a small *Syntarsus*, another crested meal-eating dinosaur. The crests of these animals were probably brightly colored and would have been used for signaling.

37

HETERODONTOSAURUS

• ORNITHOPOD • SMALL ROOTER AND BROWSER •

Most modern reptiles, such as lizards and crocodiles, have teeth that are all the same size. It is really only the mammals, such as cats, dogs, rodents, and monkeys, that have teeth organized into killing teeth, biting teeth, grinding teeth, and so on. Some of the dinosaurs, however, had different-size teeth, each with special functions.

Heterodontosaurus was one of the first of these. It had sharp teeth at the front for cutting off the leaves that it ate, long fangs at each side probably for breaking stems, and broad teeth at the back for grinding food. This is the same kind of tooth arrangement that people have! Some specimens seem to lack the fangs. Maybe only the males had them and used them for fighting.

Apart from the teeth, *Heterodontosaurus* looked very much like any other primitive two-footed plant-eating dinosaur. It would have spent most of its time on its hind legs, balanced by its long tail, like the meat eaters of the time. If you had been around, you would easily have been able to tell a two-footed plant eater from a meat eater. The plant eater would have had a much heavier body, as it needed a bigger intestine to digest its tough food. Also, nearly all the two-footed plant eaters had cheek pouches to hold the food while chewing it. The meat eaters would have had crocodile-like jaws. Like all the later two-footed plant eaters, *Heterodontosaurus* had a horny beak at the front of its mouth. Its five-fingered hands had a big-clawed thumb that could grasp the plants it ate.

▶ *Heterodontosaurus*, with its teeth of different sizes, forages for food around a dead tree at the edge of the Early Jurassic desert.

▲ *Heterodontosaurus* skeletons have been found curled up together. Perhaps they slept through the drier seasons of the year in burrows, as do some modern desert animals, such as these meerkats.

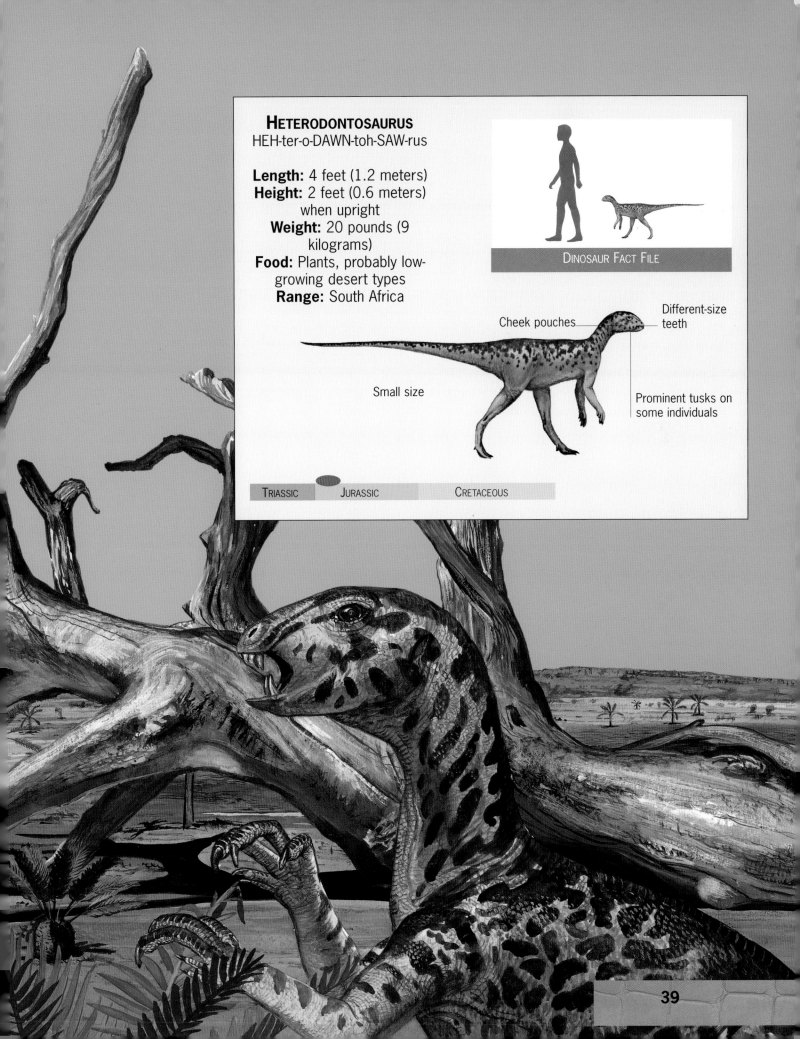

HETERODONTOSAURUS
HEH-ter-o-DAWN-toh-SAW-rus

Length: 4 feet (1.2 meters)
Height: 2 feet (0.6 meters) when upright
Weight: 20 pounds (9 kilograms)
Food: Plants, probably low-growing desert types
Range: South Africa

DINOSAUR FACT FILE

Cheek pouches

Different-size teeth

Small size

Prominent tusks on some individuals

TRIASSIC   JURASSIC   CRETACEOUS

SCUTELLOSAURUS

• THYREOPHORAN • SMALL BROWSER •

As the Age of Dinosaurs progressed, the plant-eating dinosaurs developed all kinds of techniques for escaping from the meat eaters. Some became fast runners. Others developed armor. *Scutellosaurus*, found in Early Jurassic rocks in North America, appears to be one of the first species that was both fast and armored.

It was lightly built, and although its hind legs were not as long as those of some other plant eaters of the time, it was well balanced at the hips. Its tail was thin and very long—one and a half times the length of the rest of its body. *Scutellosaurus* could easily scamper away from danger. Compared to the hind legs, the animal's forelimbs were quite long, so it looks as if *Scutellosaurus* spent most of its time down on all fours. It had tiny five-fingered clawed hands.

The most remarkable feature of this dinosaur was its armor. Parallel rows of bony studs covered its back and formed a spiky ridge from its skull to the tip of its tail. When attacked, *Scutellosaurus* may have crouched down in the soil presenting armor to its attacker. Any large meat eater that picked up the animal would get an extremely unpleasant bony mouthful.

Apart from these features, *Scutellosaurus* seems to have been very lizardlike. It was no bigger than some of the larger lizards that are alive today, and its head was quite unlike that of the other two-footed plant eaters. It lacked the cheek pouches that most of the others had. Instead, it had widely spaced leaf-shaped teeth that it used to shred its plant food. Modern iguana lizards have similar teeth for exactly the same job.

◀ In the modern world the armor of the armadillo probably comes closest to that of *Scutellosaurus*. Like the little dinosaur, the armadillo can run quite quickly when it is chased by a meat-eating animal. But if it is caught, its armor plates give it a great deal of protection.

▶ The long-tailed, knobby *Scutellosaurus* surveys the landscape, keeping an eye open for enemies. If you saw it scuttling across dry rocks or disappearing into undergrowth, you would probably think that you were looking at some kind of lizard.

SCUTELLOSAURUS
skoo-TELL-o-SAW-rus

Length: 4 feet (1.2 meters)
Height: 1 foot (0.3 meters) at hips
Weight: 20 pounds (9 kilograms)
Food: Plants
Range: Arizona

DINOSAUR FACT FILE

Rows of bony plates

Long tail

Small size

No cheek pouches

Strong forelimbs

TRIASSIC   JURASSIC   CRETACEOUS

SCELIDOSAURUS

• THYREOPHORAN • LOW BROWSER •

It is the Early Jurassic Period. A low upland ridge stretches across the area that now lies between Wales and Belgium. The vegetation that grows on the hills is the same green all over—the green of conifers and tree ferns. There are no flowers anywhere. At times big-headed *Dimorphodon* pterosaurs fly in the clear sky. In a valley, the ferns are pushed aside by a smallish knobby-looking dinosaur, *Scelidosaurus*, as it lumbers down to the stream to drink.

Big meat-eating dinosaurs were around in Early Jurassic times. The plant eaters had to beware and keep out of their way. At about this time the big plant eaters began to develop armor. *Scelidosaurus* was one of the first of the big species of armored dinosaurs.

At about the size of a small cow, *Scelidosaurus* was not really a big animal. However, it was obviously one that was too heavy to run away from its enemies. It used its armor to defend itself. The armor consisted of rows of bony knobs set into the skin of the back, running from the back of the skull down to the tip of the tail. In life, these knobs would have been sheathed in horn and were probably rather spiky. *Scelidosaurus* had legs that were fairly stout. It went around on all fours.

The main groups of armored dinosaurs did not evolve until the Middle Jurassic and Late Jurassic times. Scientists have always thought that *Scelidosaurus* must have been the ancestor of the later types. The two great armored groups

SCELIDOSAURUS
skel-IDE-o-SAW-rus

Length: 13 feet (4 meters)
Height: 3–4 feet
(1–1.2 meters) at hips
Weight: 500 pounds
(225 kilograms)
Food: Plants
Range: Southern England, with
closely related animals in Portugal
and Germany

DINOSAUR FACT FILE

Rows of conical
plates on back

Beak
Cheek
pouches

Four-footed stance

TRIASSIC — JURASSIC — CRETACEOUS

◀ The armored dinosaur *Scelidosaurus* approaches the Early Jurassic seashore. It would have carried its head close to the ground to feed on low-growing plants such as ferns, horsetails, and cycads.

were the stegosaurs, with upright plates and spines on the back, and the ankylosaurs, with horizontal shields and spikes pointing out sideways. It seems most likely that *Scelidosaurus* belonged to a group that evolved into the ankylosaurs. One reason for this thinking is that *Scelidosaurus* had its skull encased in bony plates, as had the later ankylosaurs but not the stegosaurs. But we have found no fossils of armored dinosaurs from the 40 million years between *Scelidosaurus* and the later armored types.

▶ The rhinoceros is a large, armored, stoutly built plant eater. Its armor consists of thick folds of lumpy skin. It relies on its armor in battles with other rhinoceroses for territory or for mates.

ORNITHOLESTES

•THEROPOD • SWIFT HUNTER •

On the Late Jurassic plains of western North America, herds of huge plant eaters such as *Apatosaurus* and *Brachiosaurus*, and the armored giants such as *Stegosaurus*, were stalked and killed by mighty meat eaters, among them *Allosaurus*. However, not all the dinosaurs there at that time were large monsters. There also were lightweight, nimble little meat eaters such as *Ornitholestes*.

The small mammals of the time, along with the lizards and lizardlike animals, and even hatchling dinosaurs, would have been fair game for any small jackal-size hunter. *Ornitholestes* was just such a creature, and its light build would also have given it the speed to chase down startled lizards or to escape from enraged adult dinosaurs who found their nests raided.

Ornitholestes had a body shape—long jaws and sharp teeth, long hind legs and a balancing tail—like that of the big meat eaters but on a small scale. It could use its hands well. Each hand had two very long fingers and one quite short. *Ornitholestes* could probably have used the short finger like a thumb for grasping. All three fingers had strong claws.

The skull of *Ornitholestes* was very short, which is unusual for the smaller meat-eating dinosaurs, and its lower jaw was deep and strong. This may mean that the animal killed its prey by a strong bite, as do cats, rather than by pulling it to bits with its claws.

Ornitholestes means "bird robber," but there is no evidence to show that it really did catch and eat birds.

▶ *Ornitholestes* snatches a young crocodile from its nest to eat. Having killed its prey, *Ornitholestes* probably swallowed it whole. *Ornitholestes*'s small size meant that it could hunt small fast-moving prey that was not available to the larger dinosaurs of the region.

ORNITHOLESTES
or-NITH-o-LESS-teez

Length: 6 feet (1.8 meters)
Height: 16 inches (0.4 meters) at the hips
Weight: 25 pounds (11 kilograms)
Food: Meat—probably small living things caught on the run, maybe carrion
Range: Wyoming

Small crest

Small size

Two grasping fingers and a thumb

DINOSAUR FACT FILE

TRIASSIC   JURASSIC   CRETACEOUS

ELAPHROSAURUS

• THEROPOD • FAST HUNTER •

This dinosaur was like a cheetah—long and lean, built for speed—but it ran on its hind legs. It lived on the wooded coastal plain of Tanzania in the Late Jurassic Period. Its neighbors were the huge long-necked plant eater *Brachiosaurus* and the stegosaur *Kentrosaurus*. It left these creatures alone. Instead, it hunted smaller plant eaters such as *Dryosaurus*, a relative of *Hypsilophodon*.

The lightness of *Elaphrosaurus*'s build and parts of its skeleton, particularly the front limbs, makes us think that it was related to the small meat-eating dinosaurs of Triassic and Early Jurassic times, such as *Coelophysis*. Unfortunately no skull of *Elaphrosaurus* has ever been found, and so our knowledge of this animal is incomplete.

A partial skeleton was discovered in Tanzania in the 1920s. Since then, odd bones, possibly of *Elaphrosaurus*, have been found all over northern Africa. In the 1980s, an arm bone that seems to have belonged to this beast was found in Wyoming. This suggests that *Elaphrosaurus*, as well as *Brachiosaurus* and the stegosaurs, spread all over the world before the continents broke up in the middle of the Age of Dinosaurs.

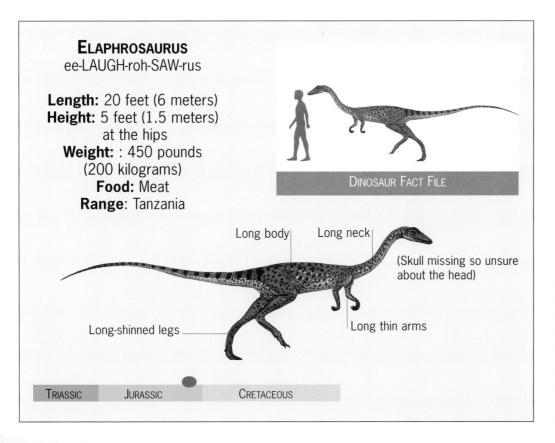

ELAPHROSAURUS
ee-LAUGH-roh-SAW-rus

Length: 20 feet (6 meters)
Height: 5 feet (1.5 meters)
at the hips
Weight: : 450 pounds
(200 kilograms)
Food: Meat
Range: Tanzania

DINOSAUR FACT FILE

Long body | Long neck

(Skull missing so unsure about the head)

Long-shinned legs

Long thin arms

| TRIASSIC | JURASSIC | CRETACEOUS |

▼ On the modern plains of Tanzania the cheetah runs down the zebra, on which it preys. Both animals are built for speed. Sometimes the cheetah wins the chase, and sometimes the zebra. Dinosaur chases would have had similar endings.

◀ Long-bodied, swift-moving *Elaphrosaurus* must have pursued the agile plant eater *Dryosaurus* through the woods and thickets of Late Jurassic Tanzania, dodging to keep its prey in sight as it ran it down.

COMPSOGNATHUS

• THEROPOD • SMALL, FAST HUNTER •

A little chicken-size creature, scampering along a shoreline, disturbs clouds of sandflies from the mounds of seaweed.

Not the image we usually have of a dinosaur, is it? Yet this is *Compsognathus*, one of the smallest and lightest dinosaurs that we know. It must have looked very much like a featherless chicken. In build and structure it was much like the first bird, *Archaeopteryx*, which lived at the same time and in the same place. This was the Late Jurassic, and the place was the island group that lay scattered across the shallow sea that covered much of northern Europe at that time.

The skeletons of *Compsognathus* discovered so far exist as fossils in thinly bedded limestone rock that developed in shallow waters long ago. The limestone was so fine that it has preserved details of the dinosaur's way of life. The most famous skeleton, found in Germany, is possibly

that of a female—little spheres in and around its skeleton were probably unlaid eggs. It still had the bones of the animal's last meal in its stomach cavity—a fast-moving long-tailed lizard, like a modern iguana. *Compsognathus* probably ate other small animals, too, such as insects and early mammals.

Now we can picture its last activities. While searching for somewhere to lay her eggs, the *Compsognathus* sees the lizard run out into the sunlight of the beach. This is too good a chance for a meal to miss. On her long hind legs she scampers after it, and after a short chase, she seizes it in her little teeth, kills it, and swallows it whole. Maybe the chase took her so far down the beach that a wave caught her and she drowned. Eventually she was carried out into the quiet waters of the lagoon, sank to the bottom, and was buried in the fine mud and fossilized.

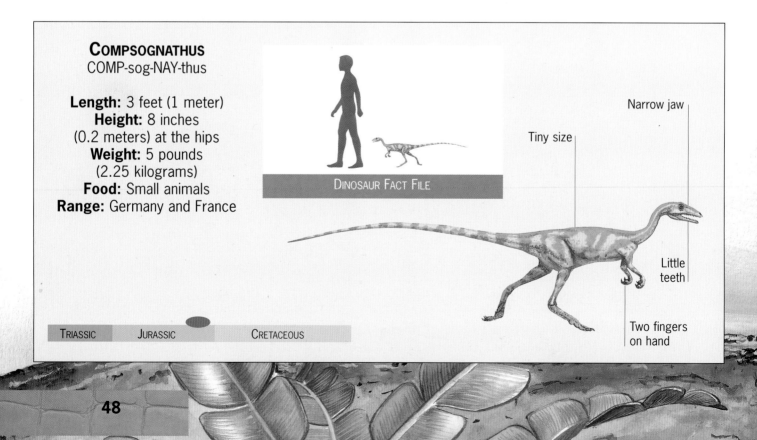

COMPSOGNATHUS
COMP-sog-NAY-thus

Length: 3 feet (1 meter)
Height: 8 inches
(0.2 meters) at the hips
Weight: 5 pounds
(2.25 kilograms)
Food: Small animals
Range: Germany and France

DINOSAUR FACT FILE

Narrow jaw

Tiny size

Little teeth

Two fingers on hand

TRIASSIC   JURASSIC   CRETACEOUS

Imagine a chicken without any feathers. Then give it a long tail and a toothy mouth. This is what *Compsognathus* looked like. One skeleton of the first bird, *Archaeopteryx*, was thought to have been that of *Compsognathus* until someone noticed there were impressions of feathers around it.

ALLOSAURUS

• THEROPOD • BIG, FIERCE HUNTER •

A 3-foot-long head, with jaws open wide and armed with sawlike teeth, bites into the thigh of a young *Camptosaurus*, ripping back the skin, tearing away flesh, and scraping along the bone. Making a panicking hiss, the animal collapses in the dust. Its attacker, an adult *Allosaurus*, lunges for the animal's throat.

Allosaurus uses the huge claw on its first finger to hook into the skin of its victim's neck. With its great mouth it bites down once more to finish the kill. The rest of the stampeding *Camptosaurus* herd slow down. Their first rush of panic is over. They forget the *Allosaurus* since it poses no danger now that it has made its kill.

The other members of the *Allosaurus* pack gather around to feast. Smaller dinosaurs, such as *Ornitholestes*, approach later, looking for an opportunity to dart in and steal a piece of meat. Perhaps pterosaurs circle above, ready to scavenge anything left over.

All this, of course, is what we think may have happened. However, we know that the big plant eaters of Late Jurassic North America were preyed upon by the huge meat eater *Allosaurus*.

In the rocks of the time are skeletons that were torn apart with great ferocity, with deep grooves in the bones scored by *Allosaurus* teeth, and with broken *Allosaurus* teeth scattered around.

ALLOSAURUS
AL-o-SAW-rus

Length: 33 feet (10 meters)
Height: about 6½ feet (2 meters)
Weight: 5.5 tons (5,000 kilograms)
Note: These figures refer to the largest species. Several species of *Allosaurus* were much smaller.
Food: Other dinosaurs
Range: Colorado, Utah, Wyoming, and Oklahoma

DINOSAUR FACT FILE

Deep head with strong saw-edged teeth

Strong jaws

Small arms with three clawed fingers

Big hind legs with three functional toes

TRIASSIC	JURASSIC	CRETACEOUS

Using its huge teeth, the enormous *Allosaurus* rips into the body of a *Camptosaurus*, an American relative of *Iguanodon*. The teeth had sawlike rear edges. They worked like steak knives, the muscles of the skull moving the upper and lower jaws back and forth, tearing the food between them. The skull and jaws could bulge outward to gulp huge chunks of meat.

51

STEGOSAURUS

• STEGOSAUR • LOW AND HIGH BROWSER •

Imagine an animal about the size of an elephant, with short front legs. Give it a little head no longer than your forearm, with narrow jaws and a beak. Give it a tail as long as its body. Now stand a double row of triangular plates along the back. These range from the size of a saucer on the neck and tail to the size of a truck wheel above its hips. Put a bunch of vicious-looking spines on the tail's tip.

You have imagined *Stegosaurus*.

This was a plant eater that lived in North America in Late Jurassic times. The plates on its back may have been covered with skin. In the hot, dry, open landscape where *Stegosaurus* lived, the wind blowing around the plates would have kept the animal cool. It used its narrow beak to probe among the prickly leaves of cycadlike plants known as cycadeoids and to nip out the tasty shoots.

▶ Dust blows across a plain in Late Jurassic Colorado. A *Stegosaurus* turns its body into the wind to cool itself. Few creatures posed a threat to the big plant eater. There were huge hunting dinosaurs about, and it must have defended itself against them with its spiked tail.

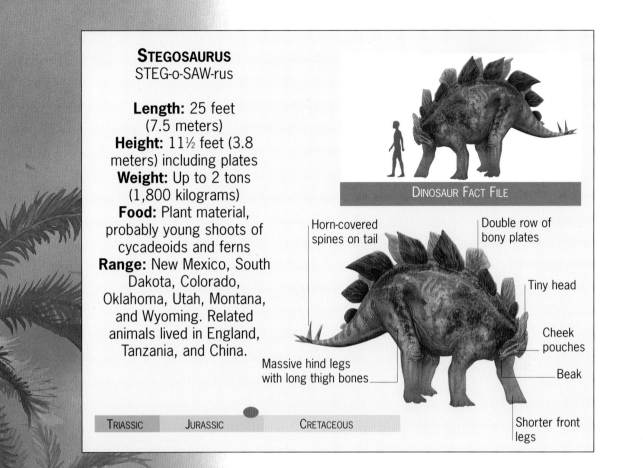

STEGOSAURUS
STEG-o-SAW-rus

Length: 25 feet (7.5 meters)
Height: 11½ feet (3.8 meters) including plates
Weight: Up to 2 tons (1,800 kilograms)
Food: Plant material, probably young shoots of cycadeoids and ferns
Range: New Mexico, South Dakota, Colorado, Oklahoma, Utah, Montana, and Wyoming. Related animals lived in England, Tanzania, and China.

DINOSAUR FACT FILE

Horn-covered spines on tail

Double row of bony plates

Tiny head

Cheek pouches

Beak

Massive hind legs with long thigh bones

Shorter front legs

TRIASSIC   JURASSIC   CRETACEOUS

Defense or display?

On the other hand, the plates may have been covered with horn and used as a defense against fierce meat-eating dinosaurs. We are still not sure what the plates did. Certainly the spikes on the tail were weapons, and the tail could be swung with a terrible force at an attacking meat eater. Beneath the narrow neck, perhaps the most vulnerable part of the animal, the throat was guarded by a kind of chain mail of little bones.

We are also unclear how the plates of *Stegosaurus* were actually arranged—in pairs, staggered in two rows, or overlapping in a single row. They may well have been brightly colored to act as signals to other dinosaurs, perhaps to attract mates.

Stegosaurus fossils are found in layers of rock that lie at the foot of the Rocky Mountains from New Mexico to South Dakota.

KENTROSAURUS

When we think of stegosaurs, we usually picture the massive *Stegosaurus* itself. However, the stegosaurs were a group of dinosaurs of various shapes and sizes. Some of them were quite small. *Kentrosaurus* was only about the size of a large cow. But it was not only its size that was special. The arrangement of plates on its back was completely different from that of *Stegosaurus*. Instead of carrying a double row of broad slabs, *Kentrosaurus* had plates that were so narrow they could be considered spines. Its name means "pointy reptile." Small and leaflike over the neck, the spines grew tall and narrow over the hips and tail. There was also a pair of sideways-pointing spines in the region of the front hips, or shoulders.

Scientists disagree over the exact purpose of the stegosaurs' plates or spines. Many think that the big broad plates of *Stegosaurus* were used for controlling the heat of the animal. The plates and spines of *Kentrosaurus* would seem to be far too narrow for this job. Maybe *Kentrosaurus*'s smaller size meant that it did not need such a complicated temperature-control system. Its plates and spines were probably used only as

armor. Only when the big stegosaurs, such as *Stegosaurus*, evolved, did these armor spines develop into heat exchangers.

A second brain or a power pack?

Another dinosaur feature that experts disagree about is a cavity, or hollow space, that lies between the hip bones of the stegosaurs. It was once thought that this housed a second brain that could control movement of the hind legs and the tail. It is more likely to have held a gland or organ—a mass of body tissue—that supplied energy to the hindparts of the animal in an emergency.

▶ *Kentrosaurus* browses in the thicket, protected from the fierce meat eaters of the time by its bladelike plates and sharp spines. Scientists at first thought the sideways-pointing spines were over the back hip, but discoveries of related dinosaurs in China show that they were over the shoulder. *Kentrosaurus* lived in the wooded riversides of Tanzania in Late Jurassic times.

KENTROSAURUS
KENT-roh-SAW-rus

Length: Up to 15 feet (4.5 meters)
Height: 3–6 feet (1–1.8 meters)
Weight: 1,000 pounds (450 kilograms)
Food: Plants
Range: Tanzania

DINOSAUR FACT FILE

Narrow plates on neck and back

Small head

Cheek pouches

Long spines on tail

Beak

TRIASSIC JURASSIC CRETACEOUS

GARGOYLEOSAURUS

• ANKYLOSAUR • LOW BROWSER •

It is the end of the Jurassic period—a time of big meat eaters such as *Allosaurus*, long-necked plant eaters such as *Apatosaurus*, and plated dinosaurs such as *Stegosaurus*. The time of *Ankylosaurus* and other armored dinosaurs is yet to come. They do not flourish until the later Cretaceous Period. Yet here, in the riverside forests of Late Jurassic North America, one seems to have arrived early. *Gargoyleosaurus* is a sheep-size animal, with a narrow head, a long stiff tail, a back covered in armor, and a series of spikes sticking out along each side. It looks out of place among the more typical dinosaurs of the Jurassic.

As the armored dinosaurs develop, they evolve into two major lines: those with a club on the end of the tail and those with spikes along the side. Both groups seem to have descended from *Gargoyleosaurus* or something like it. The armor on the back consists of broad oval plates that are hollow underneath. The spikes run down the length of the side and the tail, protecting the animal against the big meat eaters of the time. The armor of the head is fused to the bones of the skull. In these features, it is very much like the later armored dinosaurs. However, the rest of the head is quite primitive. The jaw is narrow and adapted for eating twigs. Its later cousins have broad jaws adapted for grazing on low-growing plants. The mouth of *Gargoyleosaurus* is full of little teeth; most of the later armored dinosaurs have no upper teeth at the front. Also, the later types have convoluted nasal passages for moistening dry air or for making noises. *Gargoyleosaurus* fossils do not show this feature.

Although we cannot say for certain that *Gargoyleosaurus* itself is the ancestor of the later armored dinosaurs, its early appearance and its primitive nature suggest that it may have been.

▲ Warthogs are plant eaters with defenses like those of *Gargoyleosaurus*. They use their tusks as weapons and will fight back when attacked. *Gargoyleosaurus* may have used its spikes in a similar way.

◀ Adapted to feeding on the plant life of the time, the armored dinosaur *Gargoyleosaurus* inhabits a Jurassic riverside woodland of tree ferns and conifers. This habitat is quite unlike the forest landscape of herbaceous flowering plants and broad-leaved trees that will be inhabited by its Cretaceous descendants.

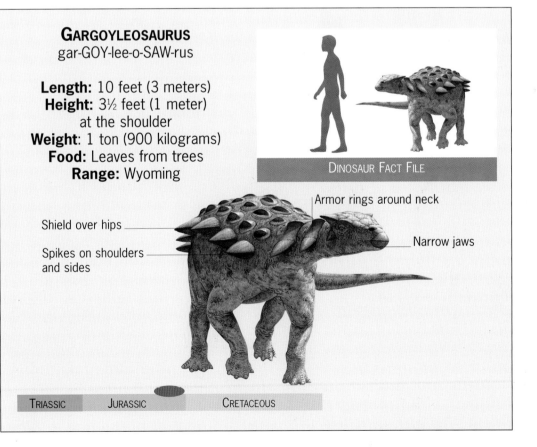

GARGOYLEOSAURUS
gar-GOY-lee-o-SAW-rus

Length: 10 feet (3 meters)
Height: 3½ feet (1 meter) at the shoulder
Weight: 1 ton (900 kilograms)
Food: Leaves from trees
Range: Wyoming

DINOSAUR FACT FILE

Armor rings around neck

Narrow jaws

Shield over hips

Spikes on shoulders and sides

TRIASSIC JURASSIC CRETACEOUS

APATOSAURUS

• SAUROPOD • LOW AND HIGH BROWSER •

Across the dry plains of the North American landscape comes a herd of huge animals. Their shapes are unclear in the clouds of dust they are kicking up. Long necks with tiny heads sway about as the mass lumbers slowly onwards—a moving mountain of flesh and dust. This is the Late Jurassic Period, the time of the largest dinosaurs. The animals are *Apatosaurus*, among the biggest land animals that ever lived.

A group of coniferous trees grows by the riverbank, shading a clump of ferns and cycadlike plants. The *Apatosaurus* herd moves from the sun-baked plains in among the trees, the dust settles, and the great beasts begin to feed.

The huge body of an *Apatosaurus* needed constant feeding. The animal must have spent most of its time eating. The skeleton of the long neck was extremely light, made of narrow strips

APATOSAURUS
a-PAT-o-SAW-rus

Length: 70 feet (21 meters)
Height: 15 feet
(4.5 meters) at the hips
Weight: 35 tons
(32,000 kilograms)
Food: Plants, probably mostly leaves and needles from the tops of trees
Range: Colorado, Oklahoma, Utah, and Wyoming

DINOSAUR FACT FILE

Long neck

Tiny head

Big claw on first finger

Elephant-like legs

Whiplike tail

Big claws on first three toes

TRIASSIC | JURASSIC | CRETACEOUS

and sheets of bone. These supported the neck just as steel beams and sheets hold up a bridge. The tiny head could swing about, allowing *Apatosaurus* to feed on low vegetation or stretch up to eat from the tops of the trees. The hips of this dinosaur were very heavy, and the hip muscles were strong enough to allow it to rear up on its hind legs for short periods.

The teeth of *Apatosaurus* were narrow and peglike, and arranged like a comb along the jaws. They raked the fronds off the fern plants and the leaves from the twigs of the high trees. There was no time for chewing. The food was swallowed as quickly as it was plucked. Down

the long throat it went until it reached the digestive system. There, it may have been ground down by means of pebbles that *Apatosaurus* swallowed from time to time for just this job.

Scientists think this is possible because they have found heaps of rounded pebbles in the stomach areas of *Apatosaurus* skeletons. Many birds use stones in this way, since they cannot chew with their beaks.

▼ A big bull *Apatosaurus* leads his family herd through the Late Jurassic woodlands. As in an elephant, the animal's massive legs supported its great weight. The feet had thick pads of gristle behind the toes that acted as cushion soles.

ARM
REPTILE

BRACHIOSAURUS

• SAUROPOD • HIGH BROWSER •

In 1900, parts of the skeleton of one of these massive dinosaurs were found in Colorado, in the same rock formation that contained the remains of *Stegosaurus*, *Apatosaurus*, *Allosaurus*, and many of the other huge Jurassic dinosaurs.

Then, seven years later, the complete skeleton of the same kind of animal was discovered in Tanzania—half the world away. It also was found along with skeletons of relatives of *Stegosaurus* and *Allosaurus*. Obviously the same kinds of animals were living in similar environments in widely separated places on Earth. In Late Jurassic times all the continents were still joined together in one big landmass, and many animals had the freedom to wander all over it.

Brachiosaurus was a truly enormous animal and like *Apatosaurus* was one that was able to browse

in the highest trees. But unlike *Apatosaurus* it did not have the muscles to allow it to rear up on its hind legs. Instead, it had very long front legs that gave it high shoulders. From this high platform the neck could reach up into the branches to browse the twigs and leaves that would have been out of the reach of other plant eaters. The top half of the animal was lightweight, with its skull and backbones made of thin strips and sheets of bone. The leg bones and ribs, however, were thick and massive. This whole structure produced a stable base from which *Brachiosaurus* could reach around for food.

▶ Held 40 feet above the ground, the tiny head of *Brachiosaurus* had nostrils that were huge. They were probably lined with moist skin that helped to keep the great body cool in the hot dry environments.

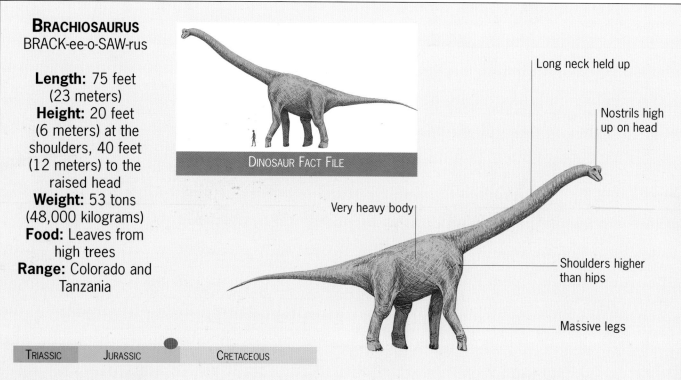

BRACHIOSAURUS
BRACK-ee-o-SAW-rus

Length: 75 feet (23 meters)
Height: 20 feet (6 meters) at the shoulders, 40 feet (12 meters) to the raised head
Weight: 53 tons (48,000 kilograms)
Food: Leaves from high trees
Range: Colorado and Tanzania

DINOSAUR FACT FILE

Long neck held up

Nostrils high up on head

Very heavy body

Shoulders higher than hips

Massive legs

TRIASSIC   JURASSIC   CRETACEOUS

BRACHYTRACHELOPAN

• SAUROPOD • LOW BROWSER •

Something is moving in the Late Jurassic forest of South America. What can it be? It seems to move like *Apatosaurus*, a long-necked plant-eating dinosaur that at this time lives far to the north. But this animal is smaller than *Apatosaurus*—only about the size of a plated animal like *Stegosaurus*. Also like *Stegosaurus* it has a short thin neck, and its head is close to the ground as the animal feeds on the undergrowth. But this creature has no plates or spikes on its back, and the tail is long and whiplike.

Although it is indeed one of the long-necked plant eaters, it is one with a strangely short neck. The head is deep in the ferny undergrowth, ripping up the low-growing plants. It has no interest in the luscious leaves on the branches above its head. Other animals will reach up and eat those.

Brachytrachelopan came as a surprise to the paleontologists who discovered it. The dinosaur was a long-necked plant eater all right, but the neck bones were short and compact, and there were only about a dozen of them. What's more, the structure of the neck bones shows that the animal could not have lifted its head far from the ground and that it would have had its nose in the undergrowth most of the time.

Most of the long-necked plant eaters raised their heads to eat the leaves from the trees above. Some of them swept their little heads from side to side in broad swaths to gather low-growing plants over a large area. They used their long necks like the hoses of vacuum cleaners. It seems that *Brachytrachelopan* was more limited in what it ate. It preferred the plants that were immediately in front of it. The long-necked plant eaters are turning out to be a much more varied group than scientists first suspected.

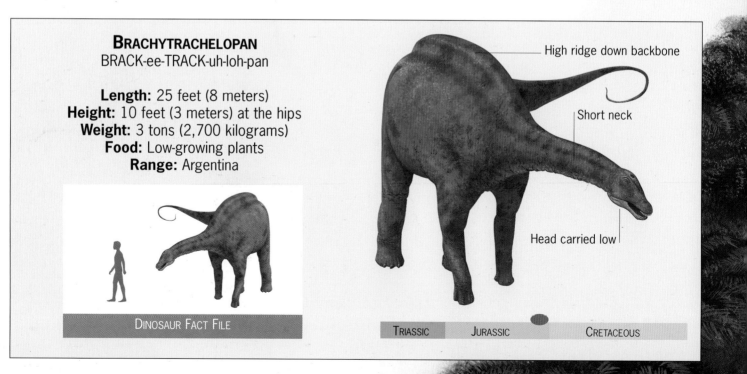

BRACHYTRACHELOPAN
BRACK-ee-TRACK-uh-loh-pan

Length: 25 feet (8 meters)
Height: 10 feet (3 meters) at the hips
Weight: 3 tons (2,700 kilograms)
Food: Low-growing plants
Range: Argentina

DINOSAUR FACT FILE

High ridge down backbone

Short neck

Head carried low

TRIASSIC — JURASSIC — CRETACEOUS

▼ Big heavy body, long whiplike tail, elephantine limbs, small head—*Brachytrachelopan* had all the obvious features of a long-necked plant-eating dinosaur, but without the long neck!

GUANLONG

• THEROPOD • SWIFT HUNTER •

Surely it cannot be a tyrannosaur? Tyrannosaurs are huge animals—some of the biggest meat eaters on Earth—just look at *Tyrannosaurus* itself. But this beast is only the size of a small ostrich!

Yet, even tyrannosaurs started small. The earliest members of the group were little, active, feather-covered hunters and lived tens of millions of years before the big ones. *Guanlong* was typical of these.

It hunted along the lakeshores of central Asia, seeking out small animals such as lizards and early mammals, avoiding the bigger prey such as plated dinosaurs. These bigger animals were preyed upon by much bigger meat eaters of the time, such as *Monolophosaurus*.

Scientists think that *Guanlong* might have been covered in feathers. *Guanlong* fossils do not show feathers. But the fossils of another small early tyrannosaur do. *Dilong* was found in lake deposits at the other end of China. It is so well preserved that its insulating covering of downy feathers has been found with it. Unlike the smaller *Dilong*, *Guanlong* had a tall crest of hollow bone on its snout. This crest was probably brightly colored and used to attract mates. Some big-beaked birds today, such as hornbills, have similar show-offy head structures. *Guanlong*'s hands were big and had three long, clawed fingers. The palms faced inward, making the hands very efficient for grabbing swift prey and holding them.

The early tyrannosaurs were not the most powerful meat eaters, but they must have been very active. As time went on, they evolved on the Asian continent. They became larger and heavier, and they hunted bigger and bigger prey. The arms became smaller as the body became heavier. The fingers were reduced

to two on each hand. After 90 million years, the animals had spread across Asia and North America, and one of the biggest and last of them, *Tyrannosaurus*, appeared at the very end of the Age of Dinosaurs.

GUANLONG
GWAN-long

Length: 10 feet (3 meters)
Height: 3 feet (1 meter) tall at the hips
Weight: 100 pounds (45 kilograms)
Food: Small animals
Range: China

Hollow crest

Feathery covering

Strong hind legs

Grasping hands

DINOSAUR FACT FILE

TRIASSIC   JURASSIC   CRETACEOUS

▶ Like *Guanlong*, the modern hornbill has a big hollow crest on the top of its head. This is used for signaling to mates and even to enemies.

▼ Along the lake shore runs the active little tyrannosaur *Guanlong*. Its name sounds different from most dinosaur names because it is taken from Chinese instead of Latin or Greek, the traditional languages of science.

CAUDIPTERYX

• THEROPOD • SMALL HUNTER OR INSECTIVORE •

Scampering through the undergrowth by the side of a lake comes a little feathered figure, rather like a spindly chicken. Like a chicken, it has wings but does not fly. As it bursts into the open, it flexes its wings, which are far too small for flying. It has a long tail with a fan of feathers at the end.

In the open it darts after a dragonfly, then turns at high speed to follow the insect as it buzzes off. The feathers of the wings and tail stabilize the animal as it makes the fast maneuvers and snaps its prey. Then it settles down. Its whole body is covered in feathers. It has no beak, but it has a short muzzle with toothy jaws. This is no chicken. It is not even a bird as we would understand it. It is a small feathered dinosaur.

Caudipteryx was one of a number of small feathered dinosaurs that lived beside this lake in ancient China. We know what it looked like because every now and then a nearby volcano would erupt, poisoning life in the area and turning the waters of the lake toxic. Any dead animal buried in the fine volcanic ash at the bottom of the lake was fossilized in such fine detail that even the tiny structures of the feather covering were preserved. If there is any true evidence that birds and dinosaurs are closely related, it is in the little feathered dinosaurs fossilized in these Chinese lake deposits.

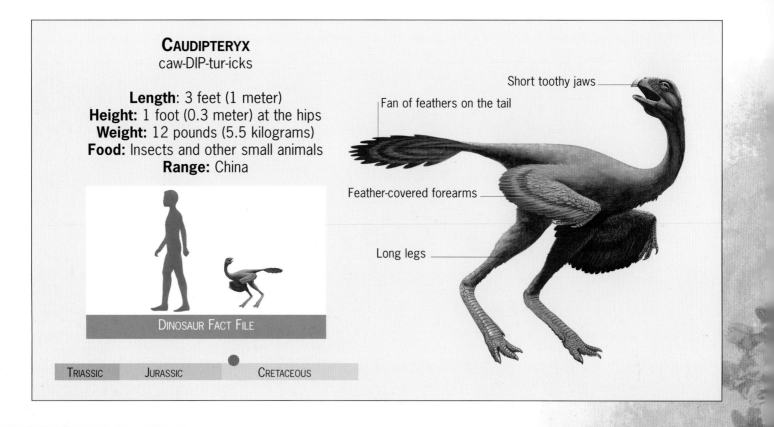

CAUDIPTERYX
caw-DIP-tur-icks

Length: 3 feet (1 meter)
Height: 1 foot (0.3 meter) at the hips
Weight: 12 pounds (5.5 kilograms)
Food: Insects and other small animals
Range: China

DINOSAUR FACT FILE

Short toothy jaws
Fan of feathers on the tail
Feather-covered forearms
Long legs

TRIASSIC	JURASSIC	CRETACEOUS

◀ The modern penguin has flightless wings, like *Caudipteryx*. Penguins use their wings for swimming.

▼ The flightless wings of *Caudipteryx* may have been used for stabilizing itself as it ran or for increasing its reach while catching insects.

BARYONYX

Although most dinosaurs fit into a few basic recognizable shapes, once in a while we discover one that is quite different. *Baryonyx* is one of these strangely shaped dinosaurs.

Baryonyx was one of the large meat-eating dinosaurs, with a low-slung body balanced at the strong hind legs by a long tail. However, the neck was held quite straight, not in an S-shape as in other meat-eating dinosaurs. The jaws were long, narrow, and full of sharp, pointed teeth, giving the head the appearance of a crocodile. The front legs were large, and the first finger, actually the thumb, carried a huge claw more than 12 inches long. The name *Baryonyx* means "heavy claw."

What could such a creature have eaten?
Some bits and pieces of the last meal were found in the stomach area of the only skeleton of *Baryonyx* to have been discovered. These were mostly the scales and bones of fish. Clearly *Baryonyx* was a fish eater—the first fish-eating dinosaur to have been identified.

We can now imagine the dinosaur crouched patiently on the banks of an Early Cretaceous stream that flowed into the great North European swamps, awaiting its prey. With a sudden lunge and a splash of water, it hooks out a large fish with its great claw and snaps it up in its mouth as the fish thrashes about on the stream bank. *Baryonyx* uses the many small teeth

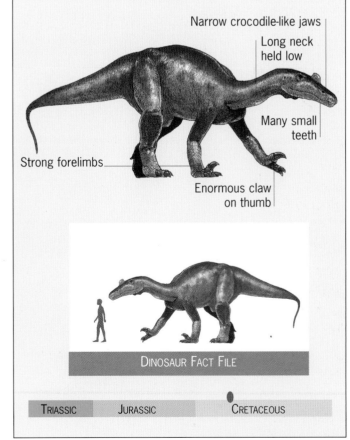

▲ In the modern world, grizzly bears gather on riverbanks when the salmon are migrating. They use their teeth or claws to catch the fish. Possibly *Baryonyx* hunted in a similar way.

◄ *Baryonyx* fishes in an Early Cretaceous shallow lake in southern England. It uses its crocodile-like jaws with 32 teeth on each side to catch prey.

BARYONYX
BEAR-ee-ON-icks

Length: 30 feet (9 meters)
Height: 12 feet (3.7 meters)
Weight: 2 tons (1,800 kilograms)
Food: Fish and probably flesh of dead animals
Range: Southern England with closely related animals in Egypt (*Spinosaurus*) and Niger (*Suchomimus*)

Narrow crocodile-like jaws

Long neck held low

Many small teeth

Strong forelimbs

Enormous claw on thumb

DINOSAUR FACT FILE

TRIASSIC   JURASSIC   CRETACEOUS

in its long jaws to hold the slippery prey firmly, then carries the fish off into the ferny shade of the conifer trees to eat.

Scientists also found bits of *Iguanodon* bone lying in the *Baryonyx* stomach cavity. We cannot really visualize this dinosaur attacking something like an *Iguanodon*. *Baryonyx* could possibly have used its big claws for killing, but its teeth are not the correct shape or size for that kind of hunting.

Perhaps *Baryonyx* was a scavenger as well as a fisher, using its long jaws to reach inside dead dinosaurs to reach the soft innards, just as vultures do today.

SPINED
REPTILE

SPINOSAURUS

• THEROPOD • HUNTER OR FISHER •

Here is a mystery. An enormous meat-eating dinosaur, among the biggest that ever lived, has a huge sail down its back and a narrow, crocodile-like head. What do we make of this?

The sail was supported by a series of long spines, each growing straight up from a backbone. Some of these spines were as tall as a person. A sail on the back is not an unheard-of feature. In modern animals we find it in basilisk lizards and water dragons, where it is used for display—for signaling to mates. *Spinosaurus* may have used its sail for the same job. If so, the sail would have been brightly colored so it could be seen from far away.

Clues but no evidence

In Permian times, before the dinosaurs evolved, there were sail-backed mammal-like reptiles. They lived in hot, dry places. Scientists think the sails were used to control the animals' temperatures. When the animals became too hot, they held the sails to the wind to cool the blood. When it was cold, they held the sails to the sun to warm themselves. This may also have been the purpose of the *Spinosaurus* sail.

The dinosaur's crocodile-like head and small teeth were like those of the closely related *Baryonyx*. This suggests that *Spinosaurus*, too, was a fish eater. However, a cooling sail would have been useful only in a hot, dry landscape, where fish would have been rare!

In any case, it is unlikely that such a huge animal could have survived on a diet consisting entirely of fish.

It is extremely difficult for scientists to make up their minds about problems like this, especially since the best remains of *Spinosaurus* to date were destroyed when the German museum that was storing them was bombed during World War II.

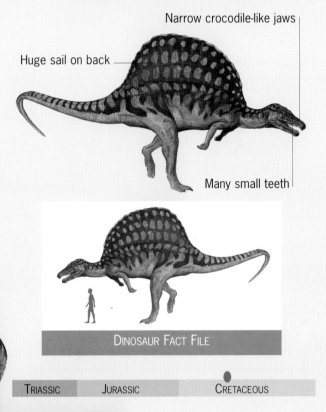

SPINOSAURUS
SPINE-o-SAW-rus

Length: 40 feet (12 meters)
Height: Maybe 9 feet (2.7 meters) at the hips, with the sail towering another 5 feet (1.5 meters) above that
Weight: 4 tons (3,600 kilograms)
Food: Other dinosaurs, fish, and smaller animals
Range: Egypt and Morocco

Narrow crocodile-like jaws

Huge sail on back

Many small teeth

DINOSAUR FACT FILE

TRIASSIC | JURASSIC | CRETACEOUS

◄ Ignoring the flesh of a small plant eater, a *Spinosaurus* slinks off to rest in the shade of the sparse vegetation of North Africa. *Spinosaurus* must have been the terror of the animal life of the time. Although the best specimen of *Spinosaurus* was destroyed, odd fragments were discovered in the Sahara Desert in the 1980s.

IGUANODON

Iguanodon was typical of the big plant-eating dinosaurs that took over from the long-necked herbivores in Early Cretaceous times. Instead of plucking and swallowing huge masses of plant materials that were then ground up by stones in the stomach, these animals were able to chew their plant food thoroughly before swallowing it. A horny beak at the front of the jaws allowed them to gather food, and strong banks of grinding teeth could shred and pulp it as it was churned about in large cheek pouches.

Herds of *Iguanodon* roamed the mires of a vast swamp that lay over much of northern Europe at that time. We can see footprints of the herds in the rocks. Now and again they wallowed in the mud of the reed beds of horsetails on which they grazed. We have found their skin prints in the same rocks.

From two-footed to all fours

There were big meat eaters around, too. They were probably on the hunt for young or weak *Iguanodon*. Skeletons of young *Iguanodon* have short front legs compared to the adults'. It seems likely that the youngsters moved about mostly on their hind legs and could defend themselves by running away from their enemies. The adults were slower, going around mostly on all fours. They had large plates of bone in the chest area that helped the front legs support the heavier body. The adults' sheer size would protect them from most attackers.

▶ *Iguanodon* browse in the thickets, sometimes walking on all fours, sometimes rising on their hind legs to pull down leafy boughs. Their hands, with three strong middle fingers, a thumb spike, and a flexible fifth finger, could be used for both walking and collecting food.

IGUANODON
ig-WA-no-don

Length: 33 feet (10 meters)
Height: 8 feet (2.4 meters) at the hips
Weight: Up to 6 tons (5,400 kilograms)
Food: Plants, particularly horsetails, ferns, and cycads

Range: England, Belgium, and Germany, with related animals in the United States and Mongolia

DINOSAUR FACT FILE

Short strong forelimbs

Beak

Cheek pouches

Horny spike on thumb

Three hooved toes

TRIASSIC | JURASSIC | CRETACEOUS

▶ Like *Iguanodon*, the modern okapi grazes vegetation in warm, moist forests. *Iguanodon* may have had a long tongue like the okapi's, which is about 16 inches long, for pulling off leaves and twigs to eat.

73

HYPSILOPHODON

• ORNITHOPOD • FAST-RUNNING BROWSER •

A small plant-eating dinosaur, built for speed so that it could escape the big meat eaters by running away across open ground—that describes *Hypsilophodon*. For a plant eater, it was very lightly built and well balanced at the hips. The legs were long and graceful, with short thighs and particularly long shinbones and toes. Most of the leg muscles worked on the short thighbone. This meant that all the weight was concentrated at the thigh and the hip, and the rest of the leg was lightweight. An arrangement like this meant that *Hypsilophodon* was a running animal like a gazelle.

Apart from that, *Hypsilophodon* must have looked like a little *Iguanodon*, the classic big plant-eating dinosaur of Early Cretaceous southern England. A sharp narrow beak would have allowed *Hypsilophodon* to select and nip out the tastiest pieces from the shoots and leaves on which it fed. It would have used its chisel-like cheek teeth to chop up the food while holding it in its cheek pouches.

The arms of *Hypsilophodon* were shorter than the legs, with hands each having five stubby fingers. These would have been ideal for grabbing and pulling food toward the mouth. Like most two-footed plant-eating dinosaurs, *Hypsilophodon* had a long tail that was stiffened by bony tendons and held straight out behind. It was used as a balancing pole while running.

On the Isle of Wight, off southern England, is a layer of rock packed with *Hypsilophodon* skeletons. Evidently a disaster overcame a herd of them. Probably they were crossing coastal mudflats and were cut off by the tide, or they were trapped in quicksand. Whatever killed them was something they could not run away from fast enough.

HYPSILOPHODON
HIP-see-LOH-foh-don

Length: 7 feet (2 meters)
Height: 3 feet (1 meter) at the hips
Weight: 50 pounds (23 kilograms)
Food: Leaves and shoots of low-growing plants
Range: Southern England

DINOSAUR FACT FILE

Light build

Beak

Cheek pouches

Running legs with short thighs and long shanks

Five fingers

TRIASSIC   JURASSIC   CRETACEOUS

▼ A group of *Hypsilophodon* trudges along in the rain. *Hypsilophodon* would have looked like the dinosaur equivalent of the gazelle. It was about the same size, and its legs were built the same way.

OURANOSAURUS

Ouranosaurus was built very much like the better-known *Iguanodon*. It had the thick plant eater's body, the strong hind limbs, and the smaller but still strong front limbs. Like *Iguanodon*, it had strange five-fingered hands. The thumb was a spike, and hooves on the middle fingers carried the animal's weight when it was on all fours. The head was like that of the duckbills, with the broadened snout. What makes *Ouranosaurus*

different is a series of broad flat spines that jutted upward from the backbone like a picket fence that ran from the shoulders to the tail.

We can visualize this animal on the open plains of North Africa, and we can visualize its picket fence covered in skin to form a kind of sail. We also can imagine that the skin is brightly colored—to make itself look bigger and more formidable to enemies

▼ As with the later duck-billed dinosaurs, *Ouranosaurus* had no teeth at the front but coarse batteries of grinding teeth at the back. The horny beak would have been used for scraping tough leaves and needles from trees, and these would have been ground to a pulp in the broad mouth.

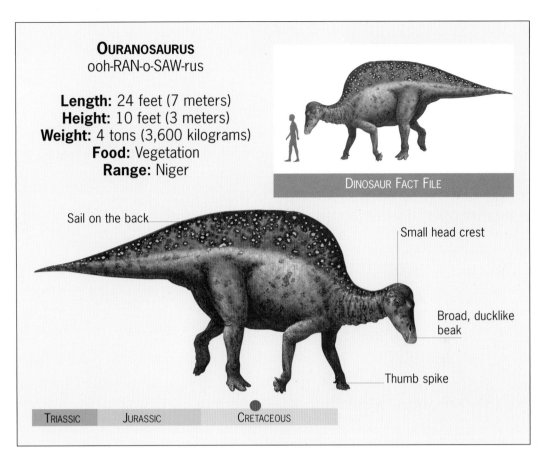

OURANOSAURUS
ooh-RAN-o-SAW-rus

Length: 24 feet (7 meters)
Height: 10 feet (3 meters)
Weight: 4 tons (3,600 kilograms)
Food: Vegetation
Range: Niger

DINOSAUR FACT FILE

Sail on the back

Small head crest

Broad, ducklike beak

Thumb spike

TRIASSIC	JURASSIC	CRETACEOUS

or to make itself more attractive to potential mates.

It also is quite possible that this sail was a heat-regulating device, absorbing heat from the sun in the early morning and giving it off to the wind in the heat of the day. In this way, the sail would have acted rather like the sail of *Spinosaurus*, which lived in the same area at about the same time.

We are only assuming that this fence was covered in skin and formed a sail. There is no direct evidence for that. It could be that the fence actually supported a fatty hump instead, as it does in a modern camel or a buffalo. Like the fatty humps on these modern animals, a similar hump on this dinosaur could have stored food energy in the seasonally dry plains where *Ouranosaurus* lived.

This shows how much there is still to find out about the lifestyles of even the dinosaurs for which we have the most complete skeletons.

SICKLE

FALCARIUS

• THEROPOD • OMNIVORE •

We often think of dinosaurs as being neatly divided into meat eaters and plant eaters. The fossilized remains show these divisions: sharp steak-knife teeth in meat eaters, coarsely serrated vegetable-grater teeth or simple leaf-gathering teeth in plant eaters; lightweight body and swift legs to help hunting in meat eaters, broad heavy body to hold plant-digesting guts in plant eaters.

These features tend to crop up in well-defined families of dinosaurs, with only the group we call the theropods having the meat-eating specializations. Ever since dinosaurs were discovered, the theropods were always thought to be the meat eaters. Yet now we know that there was a line of theropods that evolved into plant eaters. We call them the therizinosaurs.

Falcarius was one of the smallest and earliest of the therizinosaurs. We can see that it is a

▲ The fossilized remains of several dozen *Falcarius* were found together. Perhaps they lived in herds like the impala.

▶ *Falcarius*, a plant eater, has features that show that it evolved from the most ferocious of the meat-eating dinosaurs.

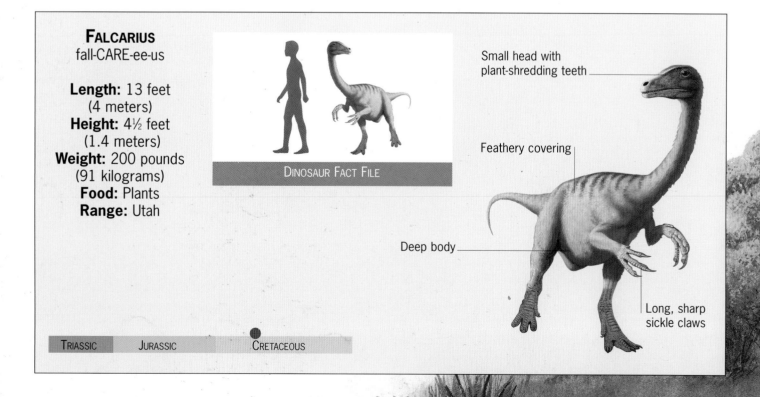

FALCARIUS
fall-CARE-ee-us

Length: 13 feet (4 meters)
Height: 4½ feet (1.4 meters)
Weight: 200 pounds (91 kilograms)
Food: Plants
Range: Utah

DINOSAUR FACT FILE

Small head with plant-shredding teeth

Feathery covering

Deep body

Long, sharp sickle claws

TRIASSIC   JURASSIC   CRETACEOUS

theropod by the shape of the skull and the hands and the feet. However, it had the plant-shredding teeth of a plant eater, and the hipbone was shaped to accommodate a big digestive system for breaking down tough plant material. Huge claws on the hands were not for killing but for ripping down foliage. *Falcarius* was close to ostrich-size, but later therizinosaurs were as big as grizzly bears. It seems likely that *Falcarius* was covered in feathers since well-preserved skeletons of other early therizinosaurs from China were definitely feathered.

And so, why did a line of the meat-eating theropods turn vegetarian? Probably because in the Early Cretaceous Period, when *Falcarius* lived, a whole new group of plants evolved—the modern flowering plants. When a new food source becomes available, something else will evolve to take advantage of it. *Falcarius* and its descendants probably did this.

AGUSTINIA

• SAUROPOD • HIGH BROWSER •

Imagine a long-necked plant-eating dinosaur—four-footed, with an elephant-like body, a small head on the end of a far-reaching neck, and a long tapering tail. So far so good. But now imagine it with a series of plates and spines along the backbone, like those of a *Stegosaurus*. Strange? Make it stranger. Place those plates so that they run sideways across the backbone, so that they face front and back rather than to the sides as in all other plated dinosaurs. This is what *Agustinia* looked like.

The plates were complex. Those over the neck looked like they were leaf-shaped. The plates over the shoulders and back were broad and ended in sideways-pointing spines. Over the hips, the plates formed pairs of long spikes. And the plates over the tail were forked. The plates were slightly curved, with the hollows facing backward. We have no idea what the plates were used for. It is possible that they were used for defense, but they would guard only the backbone from attacks from above. It is more

likely they were used for some kind of display. They may have been brightly colored. Their bases were embedded in muscle, which indicates that *Agustinia* could have wiggled them to some degree. It is tempting to imagine the animals rattling their plates together, using sound to signal one another.

Agustinia was found in South America. Scientists are still not sure about how it is related to the other long-necked plant eaters. It is probably related to *Saltasaurus*, another South American long-necked plant eater that had back armor. *Agustinia* is the only one known to have possessed such a strange array of plates.

◄ *Agustinia* is shown here with a two-tone color pattern. No one knows the colors of the dinosaurs, but some may have had patterns like this. Such colors might have helped *Agustinia* recognize its own kind and hide in the dappled light of the forests in which it fed.

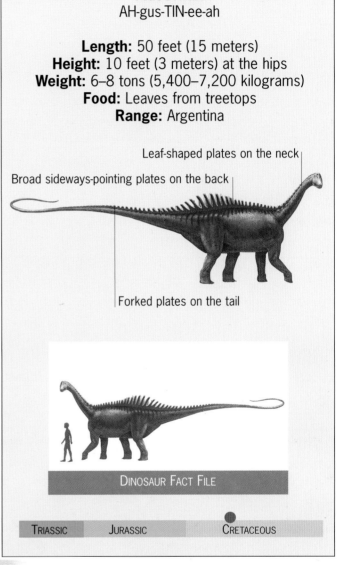

AGUSTINIA
AH-gus-TIN-ee-ah

Length: 50 feet (15 meters)
Height: 10 feet (3 meters) at the hips
Weight: 6–8 tons (5,400–7,200 kilograms)
Food: Leaves from treetops
Range: Argentina

Leaf-shaped plates on the neck

Broad sideways-pointing plates on the back

Forked plates on the tail

DINOSAUR FACT FILE

TRIASSIC	JURASSIC	CRETACEOUS

▲ The modern porcupine rattles its quills to make a warning noise.

ALVAREZSAURUS

• THEROPOD • INSECTIVORE •

Is it bird? Is it a dinosaur? It's hard to tell. It has a turkey-sized body with long running legs. Those features are common to some birds and to some dinosaurs. It is covered in feathers, which also are common to birds and some dinosaurs. Like some birds and many dinosaurs, this creature has a long neck and a small head. But it has jaws rather than a beak. That makes it more like a dinosaur. And it has a long, stiff, bony tail—another dinosaur feature. But what about those forelimbs? There are no fingers— just a single claw at the end. The limbs appear to be built more like wings than arms, but at their small size they would be of no use whatever for flying.

▼ *Alvarezsaurus* scampers through the undergrowth of the late Cretaceous South American forest, seeking out small prey such as insects and little reptiles. It may have used the big claws on its stumpy arms to help it to find food—by hacking into tree trunks or ripping into ants' nests.

To tell the truth, scientists are still not sure whether *Alvarezsaurus* should be classified as a bird or as a dinosaur. They know of several other members of the alvarezsaurid family, and these animals range from South America to central Asia. They all have those strange stumpy forelimbs with the big claw.

It is possible that the big claw was used for digging. It was certainly strong enough. Some scientists suggest that *Alvarezsaurus* may have been a kind of dinosaurian anteater, using the heavy claws to rip into termite mounds so that it could eat the insects inside. Its long legs indicate that it was a fast runner. Although it had no other defenses, it would have been able to run swiftly away from any predator.

▲ The giant anteater is of similar shape and build to *Alvarezsaurus*. It has claws for digging into anthills, a long snout for getting at its food, long legs, and a long tail.

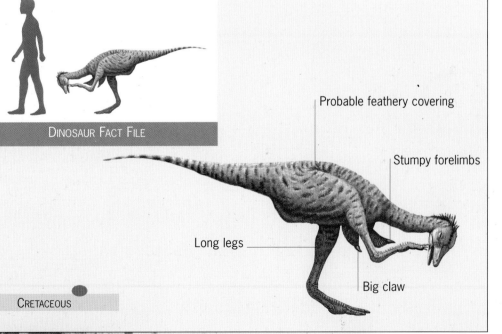

ALVAREZSAURUS
AL-vuh-rez-SAW-rus

Length: 4–6 feet
(1–2 meters)
Height: 2 feet
(0.6 meter) at the hips
Weight: 16 pounds
(7 kilograms)
Food: Possibly
insects and lizards
Range: South
America, but close
relatives in Mongolia

DINOSAUR FACT FILE

Probable feathery covering

Stumpy forelimbs

Long legs

Big claw

TRIASSIC	JURASSIC	CRETACEOUS	

SALTASAURUS

• SAUROPOD • BROWSER •

By the end of the Cretaceous Period, most of the long-necked leaf-eating dinosaurs had died out. Their places had been taken by animals such as the hadrosaurs, which ate ferns and chunks of trees with their beaks and grinding teeth. However, in some places the long-necks lived on. South America was one such place. At the end of the Cretaceous, it was an island continent, and it was inhabited by animals that lived nowhere else. This is rather like Australia today with its kangaroos, echidnas, and koalas. The beaked dinosaurs did not do especially well in South America, and the long-necked plant eaters thrived.

Saltasaurus was one of these. The amazing thing about it was that it was armored. There were many types of armored dinosaurs, but no one thought that the long-necked tree eaters

▼ *Saltasaurus* pushes its way through the Late Cretaceous vegetation, its broad back presenting a shield of solid armor to any attacker. It could rear up on its hind legs like *Apatosaurus*. It probably had a head shaped like that of *Apatosaurus*, too.

could carry armor plates. Until the discovery of *Saltasaurus* in the late 1970s, it was thought that they could defend themselves only by using their sheer size and their whiplike tails.

Saltasaurus was a member of a late-evolving sauropod group called the titanosaurids. They were mostly restricted to the continents in the southern hemisphere. Since *Saltasaurus*'s discovery it has been found that several others of the titanosaurids were armored, too.

The armor consisted of a mosaic, or jigsaw-puzzlelike pattern, of bony buttons, each about half the size of your thumbnail, and a number of saucer-size plates that may have been the bases of pointed spines.

The Late Cretaceous was a time of very large meat-eating dinosaurs. Body armor like this would have been a useful defense.

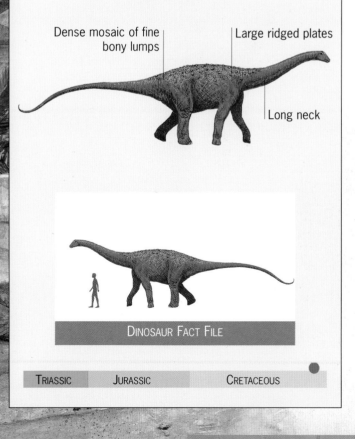

SALTASAURUS
SALT-uh-SAW-rus

Length: 40 feet (12 meters)
Height: 10 feet at the hips (3 meters)
Weight: 6–8 tons (5,400–7,200 kilograms)
Food: Leaves from treetops
Range: Argentina

Dense mosaic of fine bony lumps

Large ridged plates

Long neck

DINOSAUR FACT FILE

TRIASSIC   JURASSIC   CRETACEOUS

ARGENTINOSAURUS

• SAUROPOD • HIGH BROWSER •

Its head is bigger than a basketball, and it towers away 40 feet above the ground. Its vast neck dwarfs the trees in which it stands, being more than high enough to reach the tender twigs at the tops. Its name is *Argentinosaurus*, and it is the biggest land animal that we know.

In the Cretaceous Period, South America was a haven for strange long-necked plant-eating dinosaurs. As well as the armored forms such as *Saltasaurus*, there were truly enormous types like *Argentinosaurus*. This group of giants, called the titanosaurids because of their size, has been known since the 1920s. But in 1989 scientists uncovered the biggest dinosaur vertebrae known, each one as tall as a man. All that we know of *Argentinosaurus* are half a dozen back vertebrae, a bit of rib, and a shinbone. By comparing these with the bones of other titanosaurids, scientists have built a picture of the most enormous land animal that you can imagine.

Argentinosaurus would have had a massive body weighing about 100 tons—twenty times the weight of a modern African elephant—with a broad chest containing huge lungs. The shinbone suggests that it stood 15 feet high at the hips, and the shoulders would have been much higher. The titanosaurids grew more in height than length, with long front legs, high shoulders, and perhaps elevated necks. The tail was probably quite thick and short compared with that of the earlier whip-tailed sauropods. The whole animal would not have been much longer than some of the more lightly built long-necked plant eaters such as *Apatosaurus*.

Although *Argentinosaurus* is the largest animal currently known, there was a report of the finding of an even bigger single vertebra in Colorado in the United States in 1878. But this bone was lost soon after it was discovered, and its whereabouts remains a mystery.

Only two titanosaurid skulls have been found so far. In life, the skulls were so small and lightly built that they usually fell to pieces before being fossilized. *Argentinosaurus*'s relatives left their remains throughout the southern continents. These Cretaceous plant eaters were quite distinct from those that were so common in the earlier Jurassic Period. The titanosaurids probably started to go their own evolutionary way in Jurassic times but flourished later.

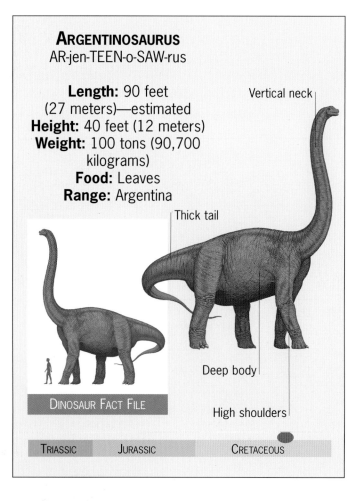

ARGENTINOSAURUS
AR-jen-TEEN-o-SAW-rus

Length: 90 feet (27 meters)—estimated
Height: 40 feet (12 meters)
Weight: 100 tons (90,700 kilograms)
Food: Leaves
Range: Argentina

Vertical neck

Thick tail

Deep body

High shoulders

DINOSAUR FACT FILE

TRIASSIC	JURASSIC	CRETACEOUS

▼ An *Argentinosaurus* walks between tall evergreens in mid-Cretaceous Argentina. In scale, it seems to match the newly arisen Andes Mountains away in the distance.

PSITTACOSAURUS

• CERATOPSIAN • BROWSER •

The head of *Psittacosaurus* was narrow and square, and had a huge beak. It looked something like the head of a parrot. That is where its name comes from: *Psittacosaurus* means "parrot-reptile." The square shape of the head was due to a ridge of bone around the back of the skull. This anchored the strong jaw muscles that gave the big beak its powerful bite. Otherwise, the body looked like that of the other small two-footed plant eaters, such as *Hypsilophodon*.

Scientists think *Psittacosaurus* belonged to a group of dinosaurs that evolved into the big-horned dinosaurs of the end of the Cretaceous Period. We can see how this came about. As the body became bigger, the animal would have gone down on all fours, bringing the head closer to the low-growing plants on which it fed. The bone arrangement in the beak is the same as that in the beaks of the horned dinosaurs. The ridge at the back of the skull would have expanded to become a frill of armor or a kind of display structure.

Some species of *Psittacosaurus* had a broad head with spines growing sideways from the cheek bones. These spines could easily have developed into horns for defense. One kind had a tiny nasal horn. It had become a typical horned dinosaur, like *Triceratops*.

▶ Recent fossils of *Psittacosaurus* show that it had a series of spines or quills on the tail. This may have been used for showing off to other animals.

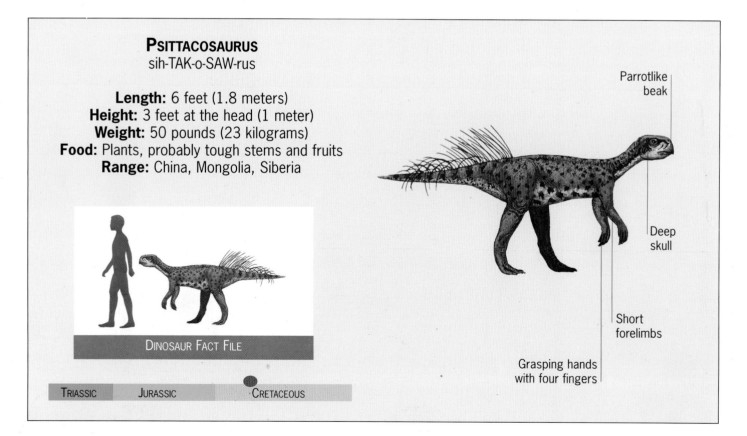

PSITTACOSAURUS
sih-TAK-o-SAW-rus

Length: 6 feet (1.8 meters)
Height: 3 feet at the head (1 meter)
Weight: 50 pounds (23 kilograms)
Food: Plants, probably tough stems and fruits
Range: China, Mongolia, Siberia

DINOSAUR FACT FILE

TRIASSIC   JURASSIC   CRETACEOUS

Parrotlike beak

Deep skull

Short forelimbs

Grasping hands with four fingers

► The beak of a modern parrot is a powerful tool. The bird can use it to break through the shells of tough nuts. By working its strong tongue along the inside of the beak, the parrot can move food about in its mouth. Maybe *Psittacosaurus* had such a tongue.

Suited for a new food source

The earliest horned dinosaurs lived in Early Cretaceous Mongolia and China, just where *Psittacosaurus* lived. Later, they migrated across to North America, the home of the great horn-bearers of the end of the Cretaceous Period.

All over the world the vegetation was changing. The cycads and fernlike plants were being replaced by the flowering plants. The big beak of *Psittacosaurus* may have evolved to cope with the woody stems and to crack the hard seeds and nuts of these new plants.

TYRANNOSAURUS

• THEROPOD • HUNTER OR SCAVENGER •

Tyrannosaurus, the "tyrant reptile," one of the biggest and heaviest of all the meat-eating dinosaurs, stalks through the modern-looking forests of oak and magnolia trees. Whiplike willow branches brush along the sides of its body, and the claws of its three-toed feet sink deep into the leaves covering the forest floor. The trees are thick with leaves in the moist soil close to the water, and the *Tyrannosaurus* is hidden among the shadows. Down by the edge of the lake are several herds of its prey. One of these is a group of *Edmontosaurus*—dinosaurs similar to *Iguanodon* but with a flattened ducklike bill. They are searching for food. The *Tyrannosaurus* silently awaits their approach.

Suddenly it charges. Pushing with its massive legs, it thrusts itself forward out of the hiding place. It holds its mouth open so its 6-inch-long teeth stick forward, and it keeps its little arms tucked out of the way against its chest. Its stiff straight tail balances its body. The noise of the crashing of the bushes and the undergrowth is frightening.

With its little eyes pointing forward, it focuses on the nearest *Edmontosaurus*. Its brain judges the distance accurately, and before the *Edmontosaurus* can move, the great jaws sweep down. *Tyrannosaurus* tears out a strip of flesh several inches deep and about 3 feet long from the plant eater's thigh. The *Edmontosaurus* collapses, slowly dying of shock and loss of blood, and the great jaws lunge again. Other members of the *Edmontosaurus* herd scatter in panic, leaving the *Tyrannosaurus* to its feast.

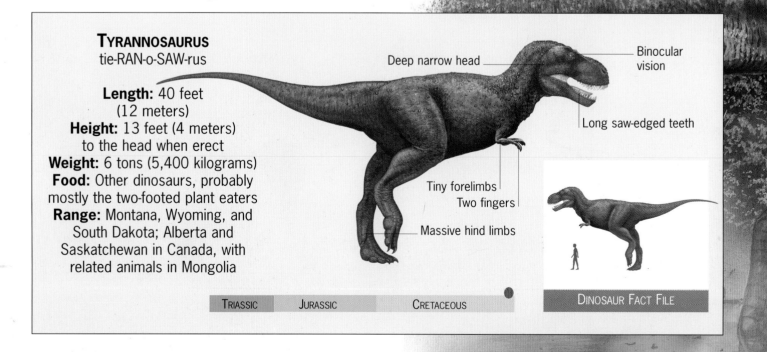

TYRANNOSAURUS
tie-RAN-o-SAW-rus

Length: 40 feet (12 meters)
Height: 13 feet (4 meters) to the head when erect
Weight: 6 tons (5,400 kilograms)
Food: Other dinosaurs, probably mostly the two-footed plant eaters
Range: Montana, Wyoming, and South Dakota; Alberta and Saskatchewan in Canada, with related animals in Mongolia

Deep narrow head

Binocular vision

Long saw-edged teeth

Tiny forelimbs
Two fingers

Massive hind limbs

TRIASSIC	JURASSIC	CRETACEOUS

DINOSAUR FACT FILE

▶ *Tyrannosaurus* hurtles in for the kill, its whole body designed for fast attack. The head and the massively muscled jaws were armed with thick strong teeth at the front for holding prey and sawlike teeth at the side for ripping flesh. Although meat eaters as big or bigger are known, such as *Giganotosaurus* and *Carcharodontosaurus*, *Tyrannosaurus* was probably the most terrible hunter that ever lived.

BIRD
MIMIC

AVIMIMUS

• THEROPOD • GRAZER •

Avimimus, or "bird-mimic," was one of the most birdlike of all dinosaurs. The eyes were big, like an owl's. The skull was deep and narrow, like a pheasant's. The legs were long, resembling those of a roadrunner. The toes were short like an ostrich's. The arms could be tucked back against the body, just as wings can be. In fact, the whole beast was so birdlike that some paleontologists think that it evolved from the first types of birds or at least some earlier flying creature. Illustrations show the dinosaur covered with feathers.

It was no bird, though. The hips of *Avimimus* were typical dinosaur hips, and its arms were too small to have been wings. The tail is missing from the only known skeleton of *Avimimus*, and some scientists think that it did not have a proper tail at all, just a bunch of long feathers as birds do. But most other scientists do not believe this since the hips are very broad and show where strong tail muscles were attached.

▼ *Avimimus* sprints across the Late Cretaceous plains of central Asia, its head bobbing and its arms tucked into its body. Built for speed, it would have outrun most of the meat-eating dinosaurs of the time.

Although *Avimimus* was related to the small meat-eating dinosaurs, it seems more likely that it ate plants. This is similar to the way that bears and pandas are related to the meat-eating dogs and cats, but they eat mostly plants. *Avimimus* had a completely different diet from its cousins. Its broad beak, like that of an ostrich, seems to have been adapted for eating low-growing vegetable matter. The long ostrichlike neck would have allowed it to reach down to the ground. A saw edge on the beak enabled it to remove plants easily from the soil.

It was clearly a running animal with legs as long as its body and neck. It must have grazed on open plains and taken to its heels as soon as one of its meat-eating relatives appeared.

Avimimus lived on the open plains of Late Cretaceous Mongolia. Footprint remains show that it may have lived in vast flocks. There, at the same time, lived small meat eaters that were fast on their feet and armed with killing claws. Such animals as *Troodon* and *Velociraptor* would have given chase, but *Avimimus* could have given them a good run.

► The modern roadrunner has a pair of legs similar in structure and shape to those of *Avimimus*. It can fly, but prefers to run, just as the smaller dinosaurs did.

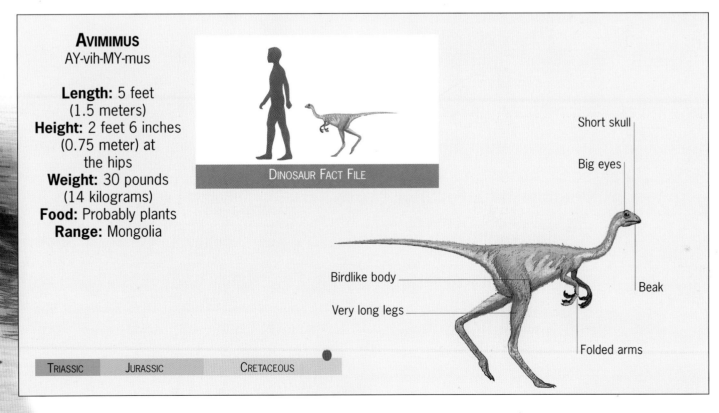

AVIMIMUS
AY-vih-MY-mus

Length: 5 feet (1.5 meters)
Height: 2 feet 6 inches (0.75 meter) at the hips
Weight: 30 pounds (14 kilograms)
Food: Probably plants
Range: Mongolia

DINOSAUR FACT FILE

Short skull

Big eyes

Birdlike body

Very long legs

Beak

Folded arms

TRIASSIC   JURASSIC   CRETACEOUS

MASIAKASAURUS

• THEROPOD • FISHER •

Have you heard of Mark Knopfler, the guitarist with the rock group Dire Straits? He has a dinosaur named after him.

In 2001, a scientific team excavated Late Cretaceous rocks in Madagascar. They filled in their spare time by listening to pop music. Then they discovered it—a jawbone with the most incredible array of snaggleteeth, quite unlike anything that had ever been found before. At first, the scientists did not even think it came from a dinosaur. Further excavation led to the discovery of almost half the skeleton (which is more than is usually found of an individual dinosaur). They called it *Masiakasaurus knopfleri*—

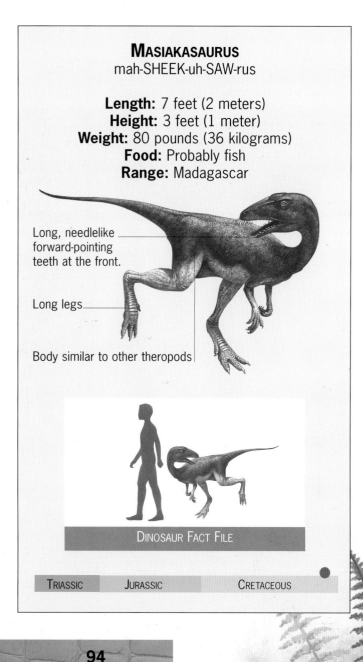

MASIAKASAURUS
mah-SHEEK-uh-SAW-rus

Length: 7 feet (2 meters)
Height: 3 feet (1 meter)
Weight: 80 pounds (36 kilograms)
Food: Probably fish
Range: Madagascar

Long, needlelike forward-pointing teeth at the front.

Long legs

Body similar to other theropods

DINOSAUR FACT FILE

TRIASSIC	JURASSIC	CRETACEOUS

▼ We find rows of long needlelike teeth in the mouths of fish-eating animals such as the gavial crocodile of India. These bristling teeth are able to pierce the slippery, scaly covering of the prey and stop it from wriggling loose and slithering away.

Masiakasaurus after the local term for a vicious animal and *knopfleri* after the guitarist.

The dinosaur turned out to be about the size of a large dog, with a longish neck and a long tail—and that incredible array of teeth. The six teeth at the front of the jaw were long, thin, and hooked. They protruded outward. The only other animals that have teeth like that are fish that eat other fish, fish-eating crocodiles, and fish-eating pterosaurs. And so, scientists think *Masiakasaurus* must have been a fish eater as well.

We can visualize *Masiakasaurus* sitting in the shade of trees on a riverbank in Cretaceous Madagascar (separated from mainland Africa even in those times) and watching its prey move about in the clear waters. Then something suitable—a fish—swims into view. *Masiakasaurus* judges its distance accurately, and with a lunge of the long neck and a snap of the toothy jaws, the slippery prey is impaled on the big teeth. *Masiakasaurus* is fed for another day.

▼ *Masiakasaurus* belonged to a group of theropods called the abelisaurids—a group that came to prominence in the Late Cretaceous, mostly in the southern hemisphere. However, *Masiakasaurus* was the only one known with this strange tooth arrangement.

MAGYAROSAURUS

• SAUROPOD • GRAZER •

At the end of the Age of Dinosaurs, there was a string of islands off the south coast of Europe. In those days there was no Mediterranean Sea, but an ocean separated the continents of Europe and Africa. Eventually, Africa would move northward and squeeze up against Europe. As it went, it would push up the mountain range of the Alps and squeeze out the ocean to form the Mediterranean, the Caspian, and the Black seas. But at the time of the dinosaurs, there were just islands and the ocean there.

The natural life on the islands was different from that on the continents. Even today, we find different animals on islands than on the big landmasses. Different living conditions exist on islands, and animals have to adapt to these differences. On islands, animals that are usually big tend to be much smaller. Because there is less to eat, small animals with smaller appetites do better. The Shetland pony of the Scottish islands, for example, is one of the smallest kinds of horse.

At the end of the Age of Dinosaurs, small versions of dinosaurs lived on these islands off the south of Europe. The long-necked plant eaters were the biggest land animals that ever lived. Yet on these islands lived *Magyarosaurus*—a miniature version. In appearance it was much like many of the later long-necked plant eaters with armor on their backs. But the body of *Magyarosaurus* was only about the size of a cow. Its long neck and long tail made up its length.

Small species of armored dinosaurs and duck-billed dinosaurs also lived on these islands.

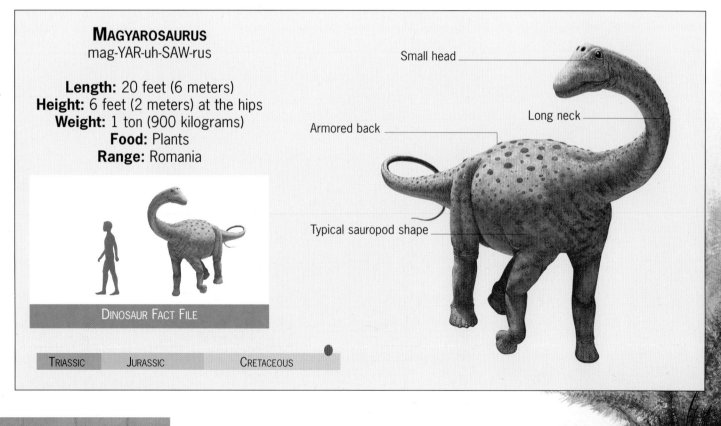

MAGYAROSAURUS
mag-YAR-uh-SAW-rus

Length: 20 feet (6 meters)
Height: 6 feet (2 meters) at the hips
Weight: 1 ton (900 kilograms)
Food: Plants
Range: Romania

DINOSAUR FACT FILE

TRIASSIC   JURASSIC   CRETACEOUS

Small head

Long neck

Armored back

Typical sauropod shape

▶ The Shetland pony is about 12 inches (30 centimeters) shorter than other horses.

▼ *Magyarosaurus* was one of the late-evolving titanosaur group, and as such it had the armor on the back that was typical of many of them. There were few big meat eaters on the islands, and the armor may have served to strengthen the backbone rather than provide defense.

STYGIMOLOCH

Imagine this dinosaur popping its head up through the undergrowth to look at you! It has a head as big as a soccer ball, with a dome on top surrounded by spikes and horns. Yet, like most other alarming-looking animals, *Stygimoloch* was a harmless plant eater.

It was a member of a group of dinosaurs that we call the boneheads or domeheads. These were mostly sheep-size animals, although the biggest species grew to about 15 feet long. They were built much like the usual two-footed plant eaters. But in head structure they were quite different. The top of the skull was very thick. In some species, including *Stygimoloch*, this thickening was enlarged into a distinct dome. It must have seemed as if each animal's skull contained a large brain. However, it was nearly all bone—and bone that was thickened in such a way as to make it extremely strong.

▲ Modern bighorn sheep have huge horns that make their heads seem much bigger than they really are. Like *Stygimoloch*, they use them for showing off and for butting their rivals.

Little brains, lots of brawn

What would a dome on the head have been used for? It seems likely that the boneheads lived in herds and that the big males fought for leadership of the herds by head-butting one another, just as male sheep and goats do today. The bones of the neck and back were arranged to withstand the shock when the head was used as a battering ram. In *Stygimoloch*, the domed head was surrounded by spines, no doubt to make the head look bigger and more frightening. A closely related bonehead, with the horns but without the dome, is called *Dracorex* ("king dragon") and has the species name *hogwartsia* (after the school in the Harry Potter books) because it looked so much like a fantasy dragon. Perhaps *Stygimoloch* and *Dracorex* rivals did not charge and crash into one another but instead locked horns and pushed.

◄ A male *Stygimoloch* rests in the shade after a head-butting contest with another male. Dome-headed dinosaurs probably had such fights to decide who would lead the herd, just as male mountain goats do today. Most of their remains that we know of consist of skulls that had been washed down from higher ground and badly worn by water before being fossilized.

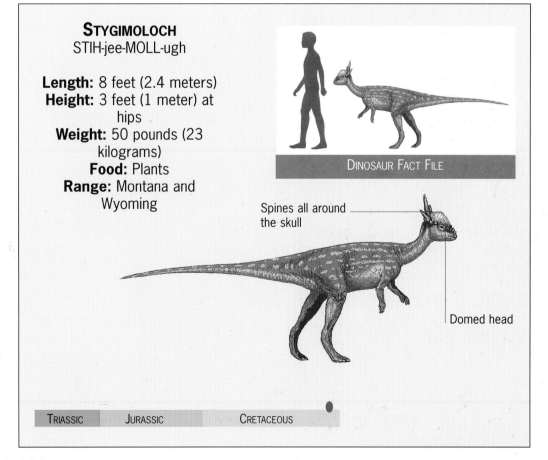

STYGIMOLOCH
STIH-jee-MOLL-ugh

Length: 8 feet (2.4 meters)
Height: 3 feet (1 meter) at hips
Weight: 50 pounds (23 kilograms)
Food: Plants
Range: Montana and Wyoming

DINOSAUR FACT FILE

Spines all around the skull

Domed head

TRIASSIC	JURASSIC	CRETACEOUS	

ACHELOUSAURUS

• CERATOPSIAN • LOW BROWSER •

Here comes a herd of horned dinosaurs. They are moving gracefully across the open plains of North America near the end of the Age of Dinosaurs. Other herds of horned dinosaurs are grazing peacefully there, too. The scene is like the plains of modern Africa, with herds of wildebeest and antelope all keeping to themselves.

As the moving herd approaches another herd, all the individuals turn and show their horns and their neck frills. Now it is clear that each herd is different. There are different sizes of frills and different arrangements of horns. Some dinosaurs have a single horn, some have three, and some have horns on the frill. Each herd is made up of a different kind of animal. The

▼A head with a rounded shield, two horns on top curled outwards, bony lumps on the nose and eyebrows—it must be *Achelousaurus*. It was named after Achelous, the mythical character whose horn was snapped off by Hercules.

dinosaurs behave like the wildebeest of today. Both wildebeest and horned dinosaurs recognize their own kind by their horns.

Each individual of the moving herd is a horned dinosaur called *Achelousaurus*. It has a pair of horns curling outward from the edge of the frill at the very top. It has no horns on the face, but it has a thick bony knob on the nose and a pair of smaller wrinkly knobs over the eyes. Otherwise, the body of the animal is almost identical to that of the other horned dinosaurs on the plain.

At the center of the herd are the youngsters. Their horns have not developed yet. The young of one herd look much like the young of any other. It appears that the different horn arrangements among these dinosaurs are important only in the adults, when they have left the safety of their family groups.

▼ Modern musk oxen defend themselves and their herds by using their horns as battering rams. *Achelousaurus* would have used its horns and bumps as weapons as well.

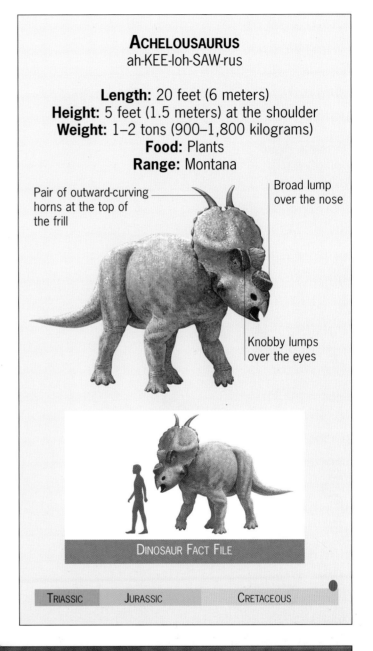

ACHELOUSAURUS
ah-KEE-loh-SAW-rus

Length: 20 feet (6 meters)
Height: 5 feet (1.5 meters) at the shoulder
Weight: 1–2 tons (900–1,800 kilograms)
Food: Plants
Range: Montana

Pair of outward-curving horns at the top of the frill

Broad lump over the nose

Knobby lumps over the eyes

DINOSAUR FACT FILE

TRIASSIC | JURASSIC | CRETACEOUS

TRICERATOPS

• CERATOPSIAN • LOW BROWSER •

▲ Like a rhinoceros, *Triceratops* turns to
face its attacker, presenting its great
horns and its armored frill. Its size and
the weapons on its face could keep any
natural enemy at bay.

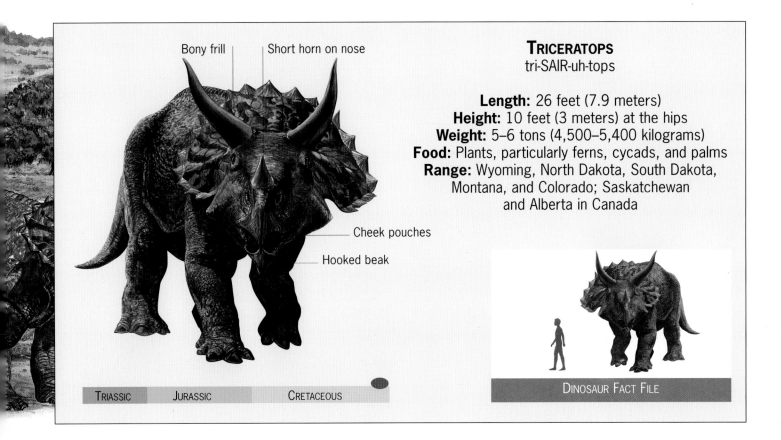

Bony frill | Short horn on nose

Cheek pouches

Hooked beak

TRIASSIC | JURASSIC | CRETACEOUS

TRICERATOPS
tri-SAIR-uh-tops

Length: 26 feet (7.9 meters)
Height: 10 feet (3 meters) at the hips
Weight: 5–6 tons (4,500–5,400 kilograms)
Food: Plants, particularly ferns, cycads, and palms
Range: Wyoming, North Dakota, South Dakota, Montana, and Colorado; Saskatchewan and Alberta in Canada

DINOSAUR FACT FILE

Three great horns jutting from an armored face. A frill of bone protecting the shoulders and neck. A body the size of an elephant. This is what an attacker would face, should it be unwise enough to attack an adult *Triceratops*.

The ceratopsians—the marginocephalians with horns on their heads—evolved in the Late Cretaceous Period. They were mostly large animals, and all had head horns and a neck frill. The ceratopsians were the last group of dinosaurs to evolve, and they lived to the very end of the Age of Dinosaurs.

Triceratops was one of the largest of the ceratopsians. There must have been many *Triceratops* around at the time. Their remains are found throughout its range. This dinosaur probably lived in herds, migrating in search of food as seasons changed. Sometimes we come across masses of ceratopsian skeletons, which suggests that a herd was washed away in a flood while trying to cross a river.

Imagining what must have been

The head of *Triceratops* was a solid mass of heavily armored bone, and so the skull is often well preserved as a fossil. This is unusual among the dinosaurs, because most dinosaur skulls are very lightly built, and they were easily broken and lost. Impressive though the skull is, it gives only part of the picture of the animal. What seem to be horns are just the bony horn cores. In life, these would have been covered by sheaths of fingernail-like material (true horn), which would have made the structures far longer than they appear on the skeleton. The animal's great beak would also have been covered with horn.

No one knows for sure what *Triceratops* ate. It did not have the squared-off mouth of a grazer. It was more suited for browsing on low-growing bushes and probably fed from flowering shrubs related to modern oaks, poplars, and sycamores. The palms and cycads of the Cretaceous period were scarce in *Triceratops*'s time and place.

ANKYLOSAURUS

• ANKYLOSAUR • LOW BROWSER •

The thyreophoran dinosaurs known as the ankylosaurs were the most heavily armored of all types. They became widespread during the Cretaceous Period, and many different types evolved toward the end of their time. *Ankylosaurus* was the biggest of them all.

The armor began at the head. The skull was a rigid box of bone, in which even the eyelids were armored bony shutters. *Ankylosaurus* means "fused reptile"—a reference to the fact that its armor plates were fused to its skull. Spines may have protected its sides. In life, these plates and spines were probably covered by horn. The broad back was protected by a mosaic of bony studs and bands of circular plates.

The tail was stiff and straight, the bones lashed together by tendons to make a rigid rod. At the end of the tail was a heavy bony club. This tail club was *Ankylosaurus's* weapon. When a big meat eater attacked, *Ankylosaurus* could swing its club with a devastating force against the legs of the attacker. (There were meat eaters such as *Tyrannosaurus* in the area.) Although most of the tail was stiff, the joints at the tail base were flexible and held powerful muscles.

▼ Startled by a hungry *Tyrannosaurus*, the *Ankylosaurus* prepares its defense. Despite the great weight of its armor, *Ankylosaurus* was agile and would have been able to react swiftly.

Ankylosaurus, and the ankylosaurs in general, had weak teeth. They could not be used much for chewing. It does not seem to have swallowed stones to grind up its food, as the long-necked plant eaters may have done. Instead, it may have had a very complicated stomach for breaking down plant food. Certainly the body was broad and barrel-like, supported by great arches of curving ribs and enormous hipbones, giving plenty of room for a large, complex digestive system. *Ankylosaurus* would have used its broad beak to pluck low-growing plants. Then it would have chopped them with its cheek teeth and swallowed the meal to be broken down by lengthy chemical processes.

ANKYLOSAURUS
AN-kee-lo-SAW-rus

Length: 25 feet (7.6 meters)
Height: 6 feet (2 meters) at hips
Weight: 2–3 tons (1,800–2,700 kilograms)
Food: Low-growing plants
Range: Wyoming, Montana; Alberta in Canada

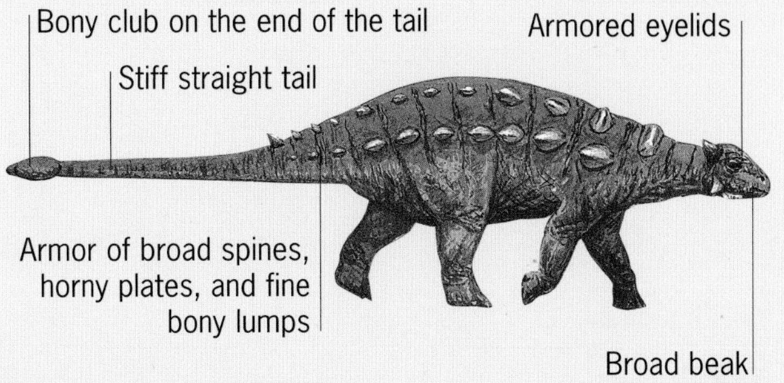

Bony club on the end of the tail

Armored eyelids

Stiff straight tail

Armor of broad spines, horny plates, and fine bony lumps

Broad beak

TRIASSIC	JURASSIC	CRETACEOUS

DINOSAUR FACT FILE

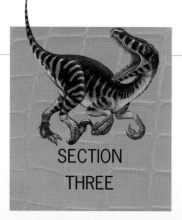

A CLOSER LOOK

• ANATOMY • SENSES • FOSSILS • DISCOVERY •

They have been dead for 65 million years. All that is left are a few bones, and those have been turned to stone by the natural workings of the Earth. How, then, do we know about the dinosaurs, these former inhabitants of our world?

We can use our imaginations. But our best understanding will be based on scientific evidence. Over the past 150 years, since dinosaurs were first recognized as an animal group, the dinosaur hunters and the scientists have been putting clues together. They find information in the rocks that contain fossils, in the bones themselves, and in comparisons with living animals.

Slowly, bit by bit, the scientists have built up a realistic picture of these great creatures of our early world. They have reconstructed the intestines inside the rib cages, put flesh on the bones, covered the bodies with skin, and placed the animals in the landscapes they inhabited. The scientists have almost made the dinosaurs live again for us.

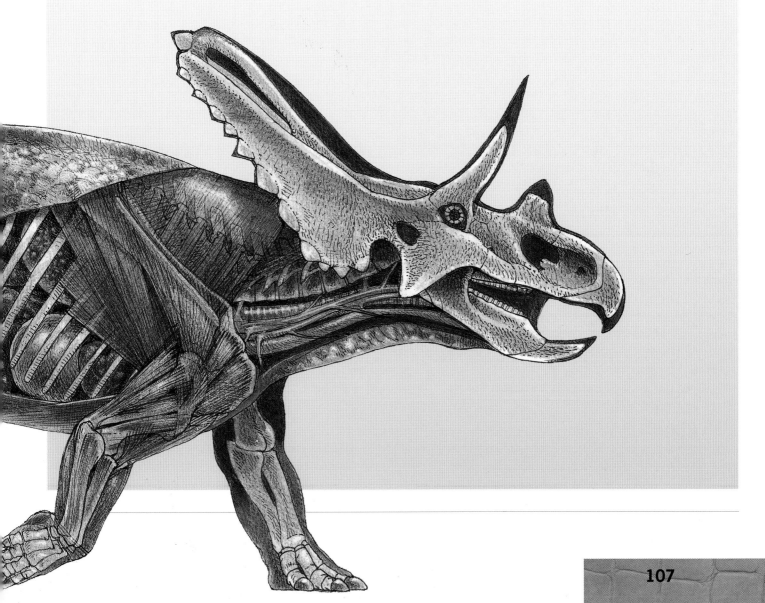

DINOSAURS WERE REAL

The Sun beats down on the dusty plain in the middle of the continent that we now call Asia. Through the scattering of conifer trees wanders a herd of the long-necked plant-eating dinosaur *Shunosaurus*. It is the end of the wet season, and the animals are migrating to find new feeding grounds. A big male steps out in front, leading the way. The youngest of the herd stay with the main group, protected by the presence of their elders. Overhead, a small flock of the toothy-jawed pterosaur *Angustinaripterus* flies toward rivers and lakes that are well stocked with fish.

▶ Using bits of evidence, we can create a picture of a herd of dinosaurs migrating through its landscape. As scientists discover new clues of life in the past, our picture comes into sharper focus.

▼ In size and feeding habits, the elephants are the nearest creatures that we have to the big plant-eating dinosaurs. The things that elephants do, such as living in family groups, give us an idea of how the dinosaurs may have lived.

How do we know these events occurred? All that we are likely to see of *Shunosaurus* is a collection of fossilized bones in a museum. Did this dinosaur really behave in this way? Was the landscape truly as it is shown here? Did these pterosaurs, flying reptiles, actually live at the same time and in the same place?

Paleontology—the study of ancient life—is full of such questions. Our knowledge of the world of the past is something like the result of a detective story. Everything that we know about it has to be pieced together until the full picture emerges. Just as important as the fossilized bones themselves are the rocks in which they are found. The type of rock can reveal what the environment was like—for instance, whether the climate was hot or cold, wet or dry.

The fossils contained in the rocks can tell us what other animals and what plants lived at the time. By comparing these extinct life forms with similar present-day living things that we know behave in certain ways or only live in certain places, the paleontologist may help us to understand how dinosaurs lived and behaved, and died, in ancient times.

DINOSAUR ANATOMY

A dinosaur, when it was alive, consisted of more than just the bones that we see in the museum. As in any other vertebrate (an animal with a backbone), the bony skeleton was just the support—the scaffolding that held the creature up. The rest consisted of soft squishy parts. First, there were the muscles that worked on the bones, pulling them like levers and allowing the animal to move.

ANATOMY OF *CHASMOSAURUS*

CUTAWAY VIEW OF THE ANATOMY OF *CHASMOSAURUS*, **A PLANT EATER**

DINOSAUR SKIN
When a dinosaur was buried quickly in mud, the mud sometimes took the impression of the skin. When the mud turned to rock, the impression was preserved, so we can see the skin texture.

The intestines and the rest of the digestive system processed the food the animal ate to produce the raw materials for growth. The lungs took in oxygen from the air. The heart and vessels circulated the blood, which carried the nutrients and oxygen throughout the body. The brain controlled the actions of the body. Next, there was the nervous system, a communications network that sent messages from the brain to the body's different parts. The senses of sight, hearing, smell, taste, touch, and balance allowed the dinosaur to detect what was going on around it and send the information to the brain. Finally, there was the skin that provided the outer covering for the whole animal.

DINOSAUR DROPPINGS
Droppings are undigested food material released from the body. Those of an ancient animal are preserved as fossils. If we know which animal produced them, we can tell what food it ate and what its digestive system was like. For example, *Tyrannosaurus* droppings full of bits of hadrosaur bone have been found.

DINOSAUR MUSCLES
If we look at a fossil dinosaur bone, we can see the ridges and roughened areas to which the muscles were attached. From these clues we can work out how big the muscles were, how they were arranged on the skeleton, and thus how the skeletal joints worked and how the animal used them to move, stand, or reach for food.

DINOSAUR SKULL
About half of all dinosaurs are known from complete fossil skulls. But often the skulls were crushed or lost completely.

DINOSAUR TEETH
Grinding teeth show a vegetable diet. Stabbing and flesh-tearing teeth indicate a meat-eater.

DINOSAUR BONES
A full set of bones (312 in *Chasmosaurus*'s case), joined together as a skeleton allowing body movement, is the best guide to the look of an ancient animal.

DINOSAUR GUTS
We can get an idea of how much food the digestive system of a dinosaur held from the volume inside its rib cage and the space in front of and below its hips. Plant eaters like the *Chasmosaurus* illustrated here have bigger stomachs and intestines than those of meat eaters so they could digest lots of tough vegetable material.

DINOSAUR FEET
The best evidence for locomotion of a dinosaur are its footprints. A set of footprints tells us how the animal walked and perhaps the speed at which it ran. We may also learn whether it went around alone or in herds. But it is often difficult to tell exactly which type of dinosaur made the prints.

Built like other beasts
All this soft matter decayed away soon after the animal's death. Often it was eaten by other animals, perhaps even other dinosaurs. Usually it was only the bones that were left behind and could become fossils.

We know that all dinosaurs had a full set of these soft parts since, as living creatures, they would not have been able to survive without them. There are no whole dinosaurs whose anatomy, or body structure, we can examine. But if we look closely enough at dinosaur remains, there are often plenty of clues that tell us what they were like.

Some animals eat plants, others eat meat— usually the flesh of the plant eaters! In the vast range of dinosaurs there were both meat eaters and plant eaters. The meat-eating dinosaurs probably evolved first, preying on other types of reptiles. The plant eaters developed from them.

As a rule, the meat eaters were two-footed animals, standing and moving around on their hind limbs. This allowed them to run quickly and catch their prey. They had big slashing teeth and grasping hands that were held forward. They were balanced at the hips by a heavy tail. All of the meat eaters, from crow-size *Microraptor* to 40-foot-long *Tyrannosaurus*, followed this design.

Plant-eating dinosaurs needed much bigger intestines than meat-eating ones in order to process more food. When the first plant eaters evolved, their heavy guts unbalanced them. The later types evolved to move around on all fours. They developed long necks that enabled them to reach around for food, and the basic shape of the long-necked plant-eating dinosaur, such as *Apatosaurus*, evolved.

Meanwhile another group of plant eaters was developing with the big guts now slung between the hind legs. These dinosaurs could still balance and walk around on two feet. *Iguanodon* and *Parasaurolophus* were two-footed plant-eating dinosaurs. Some of these two-footed species developed armor. Again, this

PLANT EATER

If you had seen a two-footed plant-eating dinosaur, you would not have mistaken it for a meat eater. Its big stomach and intestines would have given it a rather pot-bellied appearance, sometimes making the two-footed plant eater go on all fours. The head would have cheek pouches to hold vegetable matter while chewing and a beak at the front of its mouth for nipping off twigs and leaves. The plant eater would have had teeth for chopping or grinding.

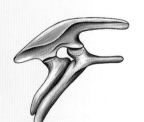

Bird-hipped plant eater

Birdlike hip bones

Skull with chopping or grinding teeth

MEAT EATER

A two-footed, lizard-hipped, meat-eating dinosaur of the same size as the two-footed plant eater opposite would have been much slimmer and more lightly built. Its head would have been much larger, and the long gash of its mouth would have shown off its series of bladelike killing teeth. Most meat eaters had fewer than five fingers on the hand. In fact, *Tyrannosaurus* had only two. The plant eaters had either four or five fingers.

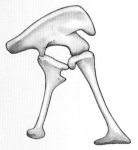

Lizard-hipped meat eater

Lizardlike hip bones

Skull with saw-edged, bladelike teeth

increased their weight and they took up a four-footed way of life. Plant eaters of this type included *Stegosaurus*, *Triceratops*, and *Euoplocephalus*.

Modern reptiles are cold-blooded. Their temperatures depend on the surroundings. By moving between sunny and shady places, reptiles can control their body temperature.

Mammals and birds, on the other hand, are warm-blooded. They can regulate the temperature of their bodies and keep themselves at the same temperature in all conditions.

Dinosaurs were thought to be cold-blooded because they were reptiles. But in the 1970s, some scientists began to argue that the dinosaurs were warm-blooded. Dinosaurs stood straight-legged, like mammals. Their rib cages were big enough to hold mammal-like hearts and lungs. And channels in some dinosaur bones looked perfect for the fast blood circulation of a warm-blooded animal.

Other scientists still regarded dinosaurs as being cold-blooded. They could not believe that a big, long-necked, plant-eating dinosaur could possibly have eaten enough food to fuel a warm-blooded lifestyle. And their bodies were so massive that they would have been able to keep in their heat in cool weather.

More recent studies of dinosaur bones

WARM- OR COLD-BLOODED?

If a small, fast-running dinosaur such as *Velociraptor* or *Caudipteryx*, below, had been warm-blooded, it would have been able to run about for a long time without tiring. If it had been cold-blooded, after any burst of activity it would have had to spend some time cooling off and resting before exerting itself again.

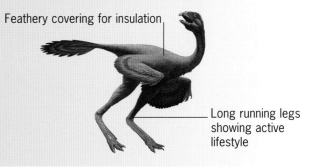
Feathery covering for insulation

Long running legs showing active lifestyle

suggest that these animals were neither warm-blooded like mammals nor cold-blooded like reptiles. It seems they were something in between. Meat eaters may have been able to regulate their temperatures, but not quite to such an extent as modern mammals and birds. Big plant eaters tended toward the other end of the range. It seems that they did not have much control over their temperatures, but they were not as cold-blooded as modern reptiles.

HEATING AND COOLING

A big, long-necked plant-eating dinosaur like *Apatosaurus* would have had such a massive body that it could have kept in its heat. Close to the surface of the animal the heat would have gone in and out through the skin, especially on the narrow parts like the neck and the tail—as it does on this lizard basking in the Sun. But in the depths of the great body the temperature would have remained the same. In the same way, water in a big kettle may still feel warm an hour after it has boiled, but the same water in a small cup cools very quickly.

DINOSAUR SENSES

◀ In the dusk, the meat eater *Troodon* snaps at a passing flying insect. We guess it could do this because the size of its brain shows that it could react quickly, and the position of its eyes means that it could focus on fast-moving prey. The big eye sockets suggest that this dinosaur was active at twilight, like an owl.

We see with our eyes, we smell with our noses, we hear through our ears, we taste with our tongues, and we feel things through the nerves in our skin. These are our senses, and with them we find out what the world around us is like. It is the same for most other animals, and it clearly would have been the same for the dinosaurs, too.

Different animals have keener senses as needed for survival. For example, dogs have a better sense of smell than we have, but we have better eyesight than rhinoceroses. It is difficult to tell how well dinosaurs' senses worked, since eyes, tongues, and other soft body parts do not fossilize. The skulls of some hunting dinosaurs, like *Troodon*, have enormous eye sockets, and so we can tell that these animals had big eyes. The position of the eyes means that they could focus both of them on the same object and therefore judge distances easily and well. Most plant-eating dinosaurs, such as *Hypsilophodon*, had eyes at the sides of their heads. This would have given them an all-round view so that they could see danger coming from any direction.

The size of the nostrils similarly can tell us about smell. Some long-necked plant eaters, for instance *Brachiosaurus*, had enormous nostrils, suggesting a good sense of smell. The small tyrannosaur *Nanotyrannus* had coils of thin bone, called turbinals, inside its nasal cavities. Modern animals with a good sense of smell have these. Separate parts of the brain control different functions. We can tell what a dinosaur's brain could do by taking a cast of the space it filled in the skull. If we find that the area for the sense of hearing is well developed compared with that for sight, then in life the animal would have relied on sound rather than vision.

HUNTING EYESIGHT

Hunting birds such as this owl have eyes that focus forward on their prey. Because the eyes are spaced apart, each eye forms a slightly different image of each object. The brain can use this information to work out the object's distance. This is referred to as stereoscopic vision, and many hunting dinosaurs, such as *Troodon*, had it. But their field of view was limited to an area directly in front of them. To see all around, they had to turn their heads.

DINOSAUR SKIN

Dinosaur skin is not preserved. Occasionally, though, where a dinosaur's dead body has been buried quickly before the skin has rotted, an impression, or mark, of the skin surface is left in the rocks. Impressions show that many kinds of dinosaurs had skin covered with scales. These were not overlapping scales, like those of most modern lizards, but tiny, horny lumps that lay close to one another, forming a jigsawlike pattern. Some dinosaurs had bigger horny plates embedded in the skin, and these were often preserved with the skeleton.

Although there is some evidence for the texture, or feel, of dinosaur skin, the color of this skin is pure guesswork. In one book you may see *Stegosaurus* with a green body with brown patches, and red and yellow plates. In another book, *Stegosaurus* will be brown above and yellow beneath, with blue plates. These differences just reflect different people's ideas about dinosaur color.

We can look at the colors in modern animals and see how each animal's color is related to its behavior. Hunting animals, such as tigers and leopards, are often striped or spotted. Animals of open country, such as antelopes, may be countershaded, having dark colors on top and light colors beneath. The youngsters of

◀ A peacock shows a colorful display of feathers to attract a peahen. We know that the dinosaurs had good eyesight and would have been able to react to such displays. Maybe dinosaurs had similar bright signaling devices, such as colorful crests, horns, or eyespots on the ends of their tails.

Club at end of tail

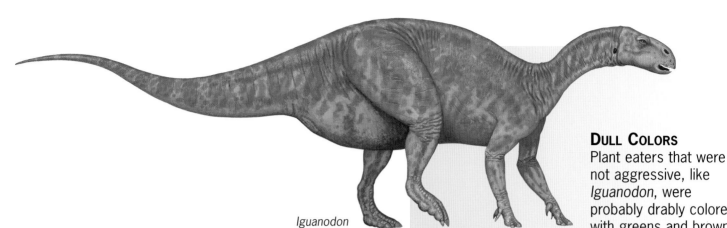

Iguanodon

DULL COLORS
Plant eaters that were not aggressive, like *Iguanodon*, were probably drably colored with greens and browns in order to blend in with their surroundings so that meat eaters would not see them.

Bony frill for protection, covered in skin and probably brightly colored for display

FLASHY SHOW
The horned-face dinosaurs, such as *Pentaceratops* and *Triceratops*, had bony frills protecting the neck.

Pentaceratops

woodland animals like deer often have fur with patches of color. These are all types of camouflage, or ways of blending in with the surroundings to be difficult to see. Very big animals like elephants, which neither hunt nor have great enemies, do not need camouflage and so are an even gray color. Similar color schemes may also have applied to the dinosaurs in their various lifestyles.

Generally, dinosaurs were probably more colorful than modern mammals since they had better color vision. They may have used their bright colors for display or as a warning.

PROTECTIVE ARMOR
The armored ankylosaurs, such as *Saichania*, had skin on the back studded with bony knobs and studs and covered with horn. Ankylosaurs are often preserved upside down in rocks formed in ancient rivers. The weight of the armored skin on the back turned the dead animal over in the water.

Bony studs | Bony horns

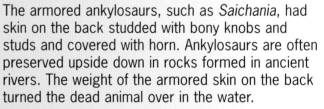

Leathery hide

Saichania

COMMUNICATION

Animals communicate with one another. They may not use words and sentences as we do, but they can make themselves sufficiently well understood for their ways of life. They can do it by visual signals, such as a peacock spreading its tail or certain types of lizards flashing their brightly colored throat flaps. The dinosaurs could probably exchange all sorts of information in this way. Animals can also communicate by smell, such as a skunk spraying a smelly liquid. We do not know for certain if dinosaurs could communicate like this, but some did have very big nostrils, which makes us believe they had a good sense of smell.

Probably the best way of communicating over a great distance is by using sound. If you have heard a cat howling at night or a guard dog barking, you know how effective this can be. Wolves hunting in a pack call to one another so that every member of the pack knows where all the others are. That way, they can work together to catch prey.

It is difficult to tell if the dinosaurs could make noises. Most animal noises are made by

CALLING OUT LOUD

Crested duckbills like these had hollow crests that could have been used to make loud noises. A flat-headed duckbill such as *Edmontosaurus* (shown on page 91) may have had an inflatable skin balloon to enable it to make a sound like a frog.

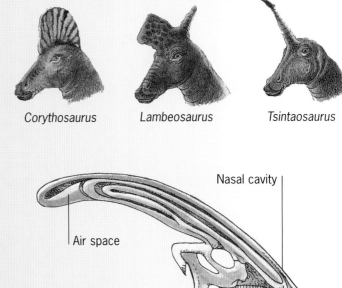

Corythosaurus   Lambeosaurus   Tsintaosaurus

Nasal cavity

Air space

Parasaurolophus

▼ The orangutan of Southeast Asia has a very loud voice. Using a voice box in its throat, it can make a noise that can be heard for almost half a mile through the rainforests. Dinosaurs may have been able to communicate with one another by making similar kinds of sounds.

◄ A herd of the long-crested duckbilled dinosaurs, *Parasaurolophus*, and another crested duckbill, a *Brachylophosaurus*, browse at the edge of the forest. The herd is spread out, with some individuals out of sight. As a big meat eater appears, the closest *Parasaurolophus* makes a noise like a horn, and all the duckbills get on their guard.

the lungs, the throat, and the vocal cords, which are soft structures that do not fossilize. However, the casts of various dinosaur brains show us that dinosaurs had good hearing. The skulls of the two-footed plant eater *Corythosaurus* have been found with the delicate ear bones still intact. These show that this dinosaur at least could hear very well.

Corythosaurus belonged to a group of dinosaurs called the duckbills. These creatures all had a strangely shaped head with a ducklike beak. Some types had a very flattened head, and some had an extravagant crest. The crests were formed from the nose bones and were full of channels that the air from the nostrils had to pass through before reaching the lungs. The channels were probably used as sounding tubes for making noises, rather like the curved and twisted tubes of musical instruments such as the trumpet and saxophone. The crested duckbills could probably communicate with one another using toots and blares that would echo through the forests.

EGG LAYING

Reptiles and birds lay eggs. It was always assumed that dinosaurs did so, too. But the first real proof of this came in the 1920s, when an American expedition to Mongolia found the remains of dinosaurs.

As well as the dinosaurs themselves, the scientists found the remains of their nests and, in them, eggs. The horned dinosaur *Protoceratops* was the most common there, and for decades the world believed these were *Protoceratops* nests. The nests were holes in the sand and contained up to 30 eggs, each about 3 inches across and 6 inches long. The eggs were arranged in the nests in spirals with their pointed ends inward.

The remains of another dinosaur, a meat eater with strange horny jaws, were also found there. This dinosaur was named *Oviraptor*, the "egg-thief," because the scientists imagined it used its jaws to rip into the hard shells of the *Protoceratops* eggs when the parents were not looking. It seemed that this animal had been overwhelmed by a sandstorm while it was raiding a nest.

Then, in the 1990s similar nests were found in Mongolia. One of the eggs was broken. The shell revealed not a baby *Protoceratops*, but a baby *Oviraptor*. The discoveries of the 1920s had been *Oviraptor* eggs and nests all the time! And to prove it, a skeleton of an *Oviraptor* was found on top of a nest. The dinosaur sat on its eggs just as we see birds doing today.

The eggs of a 40-foot-long dinosaur

Some of the largest dinosaur eggs known may belong to *Hypselosaurus*, a long-necked plant eater from France and Spain. These were not laid in nests, but in pairs in a line. It is as if the mother

INSIDE THE EGG

A dinosaur's egg, like a modern bird's, contained the baby animal and a yolk—its food supply. The whole thing was protected by a hard shell. The baby dinosaur hatched when it was able to live in the open air.

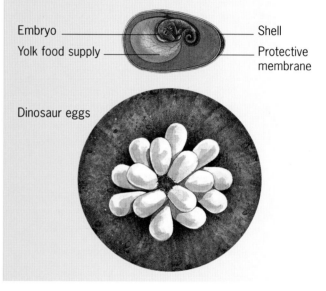

Embryo — Shell
Yolk food supply — Protective membrane

Dinosaur eggs

dinosaur had laid them while walking. The eggs are 10 inches in diameter—the size of ostrich eggs—which is small for a 40-foot dinosaur. But had the eggs been any larger, the shell would have been too thick for the babies to break out.

In the 1990s, the remains of giant ostrichlike birds were found in southern France. Scientists now wonder if these big eggs belonged to the giant birds, not to dinosaurs. The dinosaur egg mystery continues!

▶ By moonlight, a mother *Oviraptor* places leaves over her eggs. Scientists think many kinds of dinosaurs did this to help keep their eggs warm, just as some modern birds do.

FAMILY LIFE

Adult birds usually look after their young until they are old enough to leave the nest and look after themselves. It seems that dinosaurs did the same.

In the 1970s, paleontologists found the remains of a complete dinosaur nesting site in Montana. The nests were made by a type of two-footed plant eater called *Maiasaura*. This duckbill species lived in herds. Each nest would have been about 6 feet in diameter and 30 inches deep. The nests were spaced about one dinosaur length (about 30 feet) apart. In the nests were eggs, baby dinosaurs, and, most importantly, youngsters, which were about 3 feet long.

◀ Beneath a bed of twigs and leaves in a *Maiasaura* nest, the young dinosaurs hatch out. A nestful of hatchling *Maiasaura* is a wriggling mass of squawking noise. At about 12 inches long, each baby is far too small and weak to look after itself. It may have had a little horn on the nose, which would have been lost later. The baby used the horn to break out of its egg. For the first few months, the youngsters would have been fed, protected, and looked after in the nest by the adults.

The young dinosaurs had teeth that were worn from feeding, but their limb bones were too weak to have allowed them to go looking for food. This shows that the youngsters must have stayed in the nest until they were partly grown. They must have been looked after by the adults during this growing-up period.

We can imagine this nesting site as being like that of the flamingo. The young creatures live in the nests while their parents go off and find food for them. Any meat-eating animal that approaches is chased off by any parents that are still on the site.

The young dinosaurs probably remained in the nest for a few months, occasionally being led out by a parent to learn to find food for themselves. These trips would have become longer and longer, and eventually the youngsters would have been mature enough to join the herd and migrate with them.

FEEDING YOUNG CHICKS

Birds, the modern relatives of the dinosaurs, have young that must be looked after carefully. Here, an adult swallow feeds the young in a nest. Birds make all kinds of nests, ranging from holes in the ground and piles of mud to clumps of sticks in trees. We do not know of many fossil dinosaur nests. It may well be that there were several other types of dinosaur nests that we have not yet discovered.

SIZE AND LIFE-SPAN

The dinosaurs ranged from little crow-size creatures to giants more than 100 feet long. Their growth rates and life-spans were probably as varied as the dinosaurs themselves.

It is difficult to tell how old individual dinosaurs were when they died. If the bones seem to have suffered a great deal of wear and tear, we can be fairly sure that their owners were old individuals. Sometimes bones have growth rings, like those of a tree trunk. Each ring shows the growth that took place in one year.

Studies of dinosaur growth rings suggest that some of the biggest long-necked plant eaters may have reached an age of 60 years before they died. Cold-blooded animals live longer than warm-blooded ones. If the long-necked plant

eaters were purely cold-blooded, they may have reached ages of 200 years or more. Studies of the *Maiasaura* nests in Montana suggest that these two-footed plant eaters were only about 12 inches long when they hatched, but after one or two years they were 15 feet long and able to leave the nest. They would have been fully grown—30 feet long—after six to eight years.

Recent studies of growth lines in *Tyrannosaurus* rib bones show that this dinosaur grew slowly in its first few years, but then after the age of 14 it put on a teenage spurt of growth, gaining something like 4½ pounds per day, until it reached its adult size at the age of 18 years with old age and death at about 28.

CROW-SIZE

The smallest known dinosaur was the little meat-eating species *Microraptor* from China. It was about 16 inches long when fully grown. This would have made it the size of a crow.

BABY DINOSAURS

The smallest dinosaur skeleton found was about the size of a small bird's. It was called *Mussaurus*, or "mouse lizard." The skeleton lacked a tail and was only 8 inches long. It was a baby's skeleton. We know this because it had eyes, head, and feet too large for its body size. These are the most developed parts of a baby dinosaur. The adult was perhaps a long-necked plant eater about 10 feet long.

DINOSAUR FOOD

If *Apatosaurus* had been cold-blooded, it would have needed about 400 pounds of food per day. If it had been warm-blooded, it would have needed to eat close to 1,200 pounds—like this mound of food!

DINOSAUR BRAINS

A 60-foot-long *Apatosaurus* had a head that was only the size of a horse's and a brain no bigger than a cat's. Scientists used to think it had an extra brain near the hips, but there is little evidence for this idea.

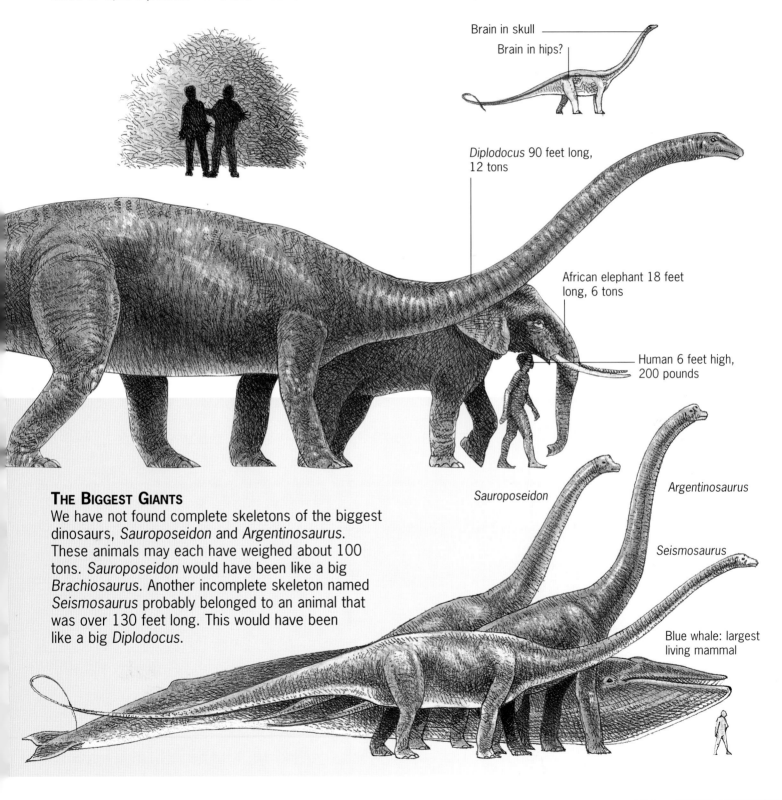

Brain in skull

Brain in hips?

Diplodocus 90 feet long, 12 tons

African elephant 18 feet long, 6 tons

Human 6 feet high, 200 pounds

Sauroposeidon

Argentinosaurus

Seismosaurus

Blue whale: largest living mammal

THE BIGGEST GIANTS

We have not found complete skeletons of the biggest dinosaurs, *Sauroposeidon* and *Argentinosaurus*. These animals may each have weighed about 100 tons. *Sauroposeidon* would have been like a big *Brachiosaurus*. Another incomplete skeleton named *Seismosaurus* probably belonged to an animal that was over 130 feet long. This would have been like a big *Diplodocus*.

GROUP LIVING AND MIGRATION

The great advantage to living in groups is safety. If there are a lot of you, an enemy will think twice before attacking. Or, the enemy may get your neighbor and not you. Dinosaurs may have lived in big herds for just these reasons.

Some of the big, long-necked plant eaters seemed to have behaved in this way. In Texas scientists studied fossil trackways made by these dinosaurs on the move. The footprints show that smaller, younger animals stayed in the middle of the herd, with the big ones on each side. Any meat eater would have to break through a barrier of adults to try to reach a youngster.

It is possible that the horned dinosaurs also lived in herds. Their remains are often found in

▲ A small herd of *Pachyrhinosaurus* crosses an old river course in a storm. The animals are unaware that rain in the hills is about to produce a flood that will gush down the river channel and drown them. The sudden death of many animals left masses of fossil bones, which we find as bone beds.

numbers large enough to suggest herding. We have seen how adult females of the two-footed plant eaters gathered in groups to lay their eggs. They may have stayed in their groups, along with their young, all their lives.

It was not just the plant eaters that went about in groups. Some of the medium-size hunters did so, too. Wolf-size *Deinonychus* probably hunted in packs. In one dinosaur find in Montana, several *Deinonychus* skeletons were found in the same rock formation as bones of a two-footed plant eater, *Tenontosaurus*. In an attack, one hunter could have gone for the victim's head while the others tore at the flesh of its belly with their big claws. The *Tenontosaurus* put up such a struggle that it killed a number of its attackers before being subdued.

FOSSIL FOOTPRINT EVIDENCE

During much of the Age of Dinosaurs there was an inland sea stretching north-south across North America. Herds of dinosaurs migrated along the western shore of this sea. They left vast deposits of footprints—megatrackways—that can be seen in Colorado.

In modern times, as the dry season starts in Tanzania, East Africa, huge herds of wildebeest migrate in search of grass to eat. Many wildebeest drown or die from injuries as they try to cross rivers.

Living as a herd

In the modern world, the musk oxen living in Greenland and northern Canada move in herds. If a wolf pack attacks the herd, the oxen form a circle with the vulnerable females and the young in the center. Usually the predators become discouraged and leave.

Migration

The horned dinosaur *Pachyrhinosaurus* used to be known from two or three skulls. Then in 1985, more skeletons of this animal were discovered in one place in Alberta, Canada—more than a thousand skeletons! In this great mass of bone were the remains of babies, partly grown individuals, and adults. A whole herd of these dinosaurs had suddenly died in one location.

There were actually too many *Pachyrhinosaurus* remains in one bed. At that place all those millions of years ago there would not have been enough food for such a big population. The most likely explanation is that the herd was migrating from one feeding ground to another and was crossing a river when a sudden flood caught the animals by surprise and drowned them.

Such events happen nowadays when huge herds of migrating animals—for example, wildebeest or caribou—have to cross rivers in their path. Many can be washed away and killed by sudden flash floods. In 1984 about 4,000 caribou perished when they were trying to cross a flooded river in Quebec, Canada.

Moving as conditions change

The bone bed in Alberta dates from near the end of the Age of Dinosaurs. At that time, the continents, the huge landmasses of the world, had broken up and were drifting apart. Each continent would have had its own cycle of seasons, from winter to summer or dry season to rainy, and the dinosaur herds would have journeyed from one place to another at certain times of the year. Another bed of this period, but in Texas, shows footprints of many long-necked plant eaters heading south. Some scientists see this, too, as evidence of dinosaur migration.

EXTINCTION

We do not really know how the dinosaurs became extinct, or died out. What we do know is that after 160 million years of success, the dinosaurs disappeared about 65 million years ago, never to be seen again.

Their disappearance could have been fairly quick, or it could have been quite slow, lasting a few million years. It is difficult to tell from the rocks laid down at the time. Many different theories have been put forward to explain their disappearance. One of the most popular theories now is that the Earth was struck by a giant meteorite or a swarm of comets at that time, causing serious changes in the climate.

COOL, THEN HOT

There is evidence of a meteorite strike 65 million years ago near present-day Mexico. After the impact, the cloud of dust would have blocked out sunlight, cooling the Earth. Once the dust had settled, the water vapor left in the atmosphere would then have produced a "greenhouse effect," heating the planet.

CHANGING SEAS

Toward the end of the Age of Dinosaurs, the shallow seas on the continents shrank. This would have led to a change in climate in which the air temperature would have risen by several degrees. The dinosaurs' body temperature–regulating systems might not have been able to cope with this.

A meteorite strike would have sent up clouds of steam and dust into the atmosphere, blocking out radiation from the Sun for months. The vegetation would have died back, and the plant-eating dinosaurs would have starved. With no prey to feed upon, the meat eaters would also have starved. When the atmosphere cleared, the vegetation would have grown back, but it would have been too late for the dinosaurs. Other, less dramatic explanations involve the steady change of the climates and the vegetation, or changes brought about by the movements of the land masses. In these cases, the dinosaurs may not have been able to evolve quickly enough to keep up with these changes.

◀ The impact of a meteorite six miles across would have pierced the Earth's crust and blasted molten rock, ash, and dust into the atmosphere.

VOLCANIC ERUPTIONS

Half of the Indian subcontinent is made up of lava erupted by volcanoes at the end of the Age of Dinosaurs. This intense volcanic activity would have blanketed the world with clouds of dust, ash, and poison gases. This would have had the same worldwide effect as a meteorite strike.

AFTER THE DINOSAURS

Whatever happened 65 million years ago, it wiped out many other animal groups as well. But some of the mammals and birds survived, and it was these that then evolved and developed to take the place of the great reptiles. Soon the Earth was alive again, and the dinosaurs no more than a memory.

CATASTROPHE

• CAUGHT IN A FLOOD • DINOSAUR GRAVEYARD •

About 140 million years ago, a broad area of swampy land lay across much of northwest Europe. To the north of it, ridges of rock stretched from present-day Wales to Belgium. The English Channel did not exist then. Streams cut ravines through the ridges, forming steep slopes of limestone, sandstone, and coal laid down nearly 200 million years earlier. The streams flowed southward toward the swamps. The ravines, slopes, and swamps were covered in forests of conifer trees. Ferns and cycads grew beneath the conifers, forming a thick undergrowth. Horsetails grew along the banks of the rivers.

This was the landscape of the dinosaurs. In the swamps roamed herds of the two-footed plant eater *Iguanodon* and its small, fast-moving relative *Hypsilophodon*. Big meat eaters such as *Baryonyx* hunted through the undergrowth. In the skies flew pterosaurs. Crocodiles and turtles wallowed in the shallow water. It was a lush landscape in which many creatures lived. Many died there as well.

Among the ravines of one of the ridges there was a depression, a giant dip in the ground. This was frequently washed by flash floods following rainstorms. During one such flood, an *Iguanodon* was caught and drowned by the waters while crossing the river farther up, and its dead body was washed into the depression. In a later flood, another dead *Iguanodon* was washed down, and its body settled beside the first. Eventually so many dead bodies of *Iguanodon* had gathered that the giant dip became a true dinosaur graveyard.

► An *Iguanodon* is carried down a gorge by a flash flood as other *Iguanodon* look on. It drowns and its body settles in a depression. This was the first part of the process that turned the dinosaur into remains preserved in rock—into fossils—that we can see today.

LOCATION OF THE GRAVEYARD

In the early Cretaceous Period, northern North America was joined to Europe, and a sea called the Tethys separated Europe and Africa. On the northern European continent there was a low-lying area of swamps and lakes giving rise to the so-called Wealden deposits. Among the swamps roamed *Iguanodon* and other dinosaurs.

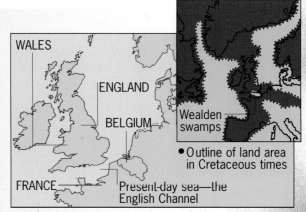

WALES

ENGLAND

BELGIUM

Wealden swamps

FRANCE

• Outline of land area in Cretaceous times

• Present-day sea—the English Channel

TIME PASSES

Within a few weeks, the soft parts of the dead *Iguanodon*—skin, muscles, hearts, brains, lungs, stomachs, and so on—rotted away. But the bones did not. They stayed unchanged and still joined together as skeletons. The river covered them with layers of mud, sand, and soil.

Over thousands of years the landscape changed. The whole area subsided, and sediments washed down from the surrounding hills built up on the surface. The skeletons became buried more deeply. The overlying weight compressed the bones and the surrounding sediments. Percolating groundwater, seeping through the sediments, deposited its dissolved minerals, such as silica and calcium carbonate, in the spaces between the sediment particles, cementing them together

and turning them into solid rock.

In the *Iguanodon* bones, changes began to take place. About two-thirds of a bone's volume is made up of minerals, such as calcium phosphate. This part of the bone remained intact. The other third of the bone was made up of proteins, fats, and other organic matter—the substance that was actually living matter when the animal was alive. This organic part decayed away and was replaced by minerals from the groundwater. The replacement took place molecule by molecule, and the original microscopic structure of the bone was preserved. In addition to silica and calcium carbonate, these minerals included iron pyrite, a kind of iron ore. Eventually the entire bone became a mass of mineral—a fossil.

▼ *Iguanodon* bodies washed down from the surrounding hills formed a dinosaur graveyard that was to remain hidden for millions of years.

THE CONDITION OF THE FIND

The dinosaur finds that give the most information are articulated skeletons—those with the bones still joined together in the positions they would have had in life. More common is the associated skeleton—a jumble of loose bones that obviously come from the same animal. An isolated bone is just a single bone. Scraps of fossil bone that have no scientific value are referred to as float.

TURNING DINOSAURS INTO ROCKS

The body of a dead *Iguanodon* settles on the bottom of a river (1). It is buried by the mud and sand washed down, and its flesh rots away (2). Eventually other layers of sediment pile up above it. Forces and pressures within the crust, the skin of the Earth, turn these layers into beds of rock, and the bones are filled with minerals (3). Now the fossil skeleton lies hidden in the rocks below our feet (4). The whole process of fossilization takes millions of years. Rock that is made up almost entirely of fossil bones is called a bone bed.

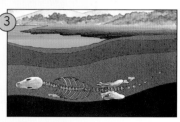

133

THE CHANGING LAND

• FIRST FOSSIL FINDS • DINOSAURIA •

▼ The small town of Bernissart in southwest Belgium in the 1870s. This cutaway view of the coal mine shows elevator shafts and passages cut through the layers of rock to reach the coal. There are also objects buried in the rocks: the *Iguanodon* remains.

It has been 130 million years since the *Iguanodon* bodies were buried. The ridge of rocks with the *Iguanodon* graveyard in the gorge was worn down by the weather, and a sea of warm water spread over the whole area. The continents kept moving, and Africa began to push against Europe. In northern Europe this movement raised the land, and the shallow sea drained away. Forests grew everywhere, but as the climate changed, these gave way to grasslands. By this time North America had broken away from Europe and the Atlantic Ocean had formed between them. Finally, in the last 2 million years or so, the landscape became as it is today.

While this was happening, the animal life also changed. The dinosaurs died out, and the mammals took their place.

About 250,000 years ago, one particular species of mammal, humans, moved into the area. As people began to explore the natural world, they developed ideas about how rocks were formed and how the shells and bones of living things of the past were turned to stone and became embedded in them.

The first recognizable dinosaur bones were discovered in southern England early in the nineteenth century. In 1824, the first scientific description of a dinosaur was written. William Buckland of Oxford University named the big meat eater *Megalosaurus*, meaning "great lizard." In 1825, an English country doctor named Gideon Mantell made a second dinosaur discovery—*Iguanodon*. But this, too, was in England, not at the *Iguanodon* graveyard in Belgium.

In 1842, British scientist Sir Richard Owen gave this group of new animals the name Dinosauria, meaning "terrible lizards."

TRIASSIC–LOWER JURASSIC DESERTS AND OASES: SOUTH AFRICA

Taphonomy is the study of what happens to animals after they have died and before they become fossils. At any site, animal remains are buried in a variety of ways depending on the conditions. As a result, we now find many types of fossils. Here is a taphonomy story from present-day South Africa of dinosaurs from the Triassic to Lower Jurassic periods.

LABELS
1. Oasis—an area of water that attracts desert animals
2. *Plateosaurus*
3. *Liliensternus*
4. Crocodile-like *Nicrosaurus*
5. Shifting sand dunes
6. *Coelophysis*
7. Fossilized dinosaur nests overwhelmed by sand

A. DEATH BY PREDATION
Plateosaurus was trapped in quicksand. Its struggles attracted small meat-eating dinosaurs such as *Liliensternus* and crocodile-like animals that tore it to bits.

B. INDIVIDUAL BONES AND TRACE FOSSILS
The small dinosaurs and crocodile-like animals that attacked the *Plateosaurus* and scavenged its dead body left behind their footprints and some loose teeth.

C. ASSOCIATED SKELETON
A *Plateosaurus* that was trapped in the mud left behind its upright leg bones. Other parts of its skeleton were scattered over a wide area.

D. DEATH BY DROUGHT
Articulated skeletons of *Coelophysis* curled up on mudstone show that these animals died when a water hole dried up.

E. DEATH BY BURIAL
Dinosaurs, such as *Coelophysis*, caught in the open and overwhelmed by a sandstorm before finding shelter, resulted in articulated skeletons lying along the slope of a sand dune.

AWAITING DISCOVERY

▲ Miners discover strange shapes in the coal seam in 1878. They did not realize it but they had stumbled upon the best dinosaur site that had yet been found.

The idea of dinosaurs became very popular in nineteenth-century Europe. The work of fossil hunters William Buckland on *Megalosaurus* and Gideon Mantell on *Iguanodon* caught the public's imagination. In natural history books made at the time, illustrations of both these dinosaurs, shown as giant lizards, were often included. So, too, were illustrations of fossil sea reptiles. These extinct creatures had been known for a number of years.

More evidence, new interpretations

The idea that dinosaurs were lizards built like elephants remained for some time. Then, in 1858, part of a dinosaur skeleton was found in New Jersey in the United States. It was studied by Joseph Leidy, professor of anatomy at the University of Pennsylvania, and he named it *Hadrosaurus*, meaning "thick lizard." It was similar to *Iguanodon*, but there was enough of the

skeleton to show that it had not resembled an elephant-like lizard. Instead, it must have looked more like a kangaroo. *Hadrosaurus* stood on its long hind legs with its shorter front legs dangling before it.

In 1868, sculptor Benjamin Waterhouse Hawkins mounted the *Hadrosaurus* skeleton for Leidy at the Academy of Natural Sciences in Philadelphia, Pennsylvania—the first mounted dinosaur skeleton ever exhibited.

Shortly afterward, in 1878, coal miners in Bernissart, Belgium, were tunneling through a coal seam when the coal suddenly gave out. Instead of coal they found clay filled with strange-looking lumps. The *Iguanodon* graveyard had been discovered.

JURASSIC PLAINS: WESTERN NORTH AMERICA

The most famous Jurassic dinosaur sites in North America are found in the Morrison Formation—rocks formed on a dry plain between a mountain range and a shallow sea that lay in the Midwest. The rocks consist of sandstones, shales, and limestones. Fossils found at the sites allow paleontologists to build up pictures of life in dinosaur times. Here are some examples:

A. SEDIMENTS
Flood plain deposits are churned up by dinosaur trackways. There are layers of limestone lumps formed by ground water; beds of limestone from the alkaline ponds; and sandstone in river channels.

B. MIGRATION
Herds of plant eaters migrating during the dry season, avoiding stagnant ponds of salty water while searching for new feeding sites, and breaking up the soil underfoot.

C. RIVERBANKS
Raised riverbanks, clothed in vegetation, where the animals feed. Meat-eating dinosaurs eat the plant eaters, either killing them or scavenging the already-dead corpses.

D. RIVER
Raised riverbanks. Water transports dead animals during the wet season, sometimes jamming the bodies together where the current drops or the river vanishes in the dry season.

LABELS
1. *Apatosaurus* herd
2. *Diplodocus*
3. *Brachiosaurus*
4. *Allosaurus* eating a *Stegosaurus*
5. *Stegosaurus* remains—associated skeleton
6. *Diplodocus* skeleton forming a logjam—articulated and associated skeletons

E. WATERING HOLE
Animals gather around a freshwater pond, filled by a spring leaking through the riverbank.

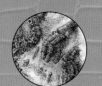

FINISHING THE PUZZLE

THE *IGUANODON* STORY:
PART FIVE

• DINOSAUR MUSEUMS • DESCRIBING *IGUANODON* •

The Belgian coal miner Jules Creteur, who found the oddly shaped lumps in the Bernissart mine, brought them to the surface and examined them. He found that they were bits of fossilized bone. Creteur had been tunneling through the rocks of the ancient ridge and had discovered the depression filled with Cretaceous sediments and the *Iguanodon* graveyard.

Mining work was stopped. A team from the Royal Museum of Natural History in Brussels was brought in, and experts began to dig out the skeletons. In three years, thirty-nine *Iguanodon* skeletons were brought up to the surface of the mine. These were mostly complete, unlike the earlier *Iguanodon* finds in England.

The scientist best known for the dinosaur

work done at Bernissart is Louis Dollo of the Royal Museum of Natural History in Brussels. In 1882, he began to study and reconstruct the skeletons. In Brussels, in a building that was once a chapel, he and his team mounted eleven of the most complete skeletons in lifelike poses. This job took thirty years. Dollo believed that *Iguanodon* probably moved about on its hind legs, unlike the modern iguana. The Belgian king at that time, Leopold II, visited the display and remarked that the *Iguanodon*, with their tall necks and small heads, looked like giraffes. In any case, the skeletons suggested an animal that was very different from the elephant-like lizards drawn by Gideon Mantell.

Dollo found that there were two different sizes of *Iguanodon*. He thought these may have represented two different species or types, or perhaps the males and females of just one species. We now believe that the first explanation was correct: there are several *Iguanodon* species.

▶ The *Iguanodon* fossils embedded in rock were in the forms of articulated skeletons. They were brought to the surface in blocks, and their original positions were plotted before the bones were extracted and mounted.

FORMATION OF A LATE CRETACEOUS BONE BED: ALBERTA

In some sites, masses of loose bones from many individuals of the same species are found crammed together. This occurrence is known as a bone bed and is the result of a herd of animals being killed and buried at the same time. Here are some examples of how this may have happened.

LABELS
1. *Centrosaurus*
2. *Styracosaurus*
3. *Albertosaurus* attacking herd
4. *Albertosaurus* scavenging corpses
5. Flood plain deposits
6. Old river channels with current-bedded sand
7. *Centrosaurus* bone bed on the bottom of river channel

A. ON THE MOVE
Herds of horned dinosaurs cross the open plain. Members of each species keep to their own herds and avoid the others, recognizing one another by the horn arrangement and frill color.

B. TRAGEDY
As a herd crosses a river, a sudden flood catches it and many individuals are washed away and drowned.

C. WASHED UP
Dead dinosaurs are washed up on the inside bank of a river bend. There they are scavenged by meat eaters.

D. REMAINS DEPOSITED
Further flooding washes away the remaining bones and deposits them on the bed of the river, lining up the bones in the direction of the current.

E. BONE BED
Masses of dinosaur bones fossilized on the bottom of a river channel, showing signs of chewing and water transport—all are about the same size and aligned in the same direction.

DINOSAUR FEVER

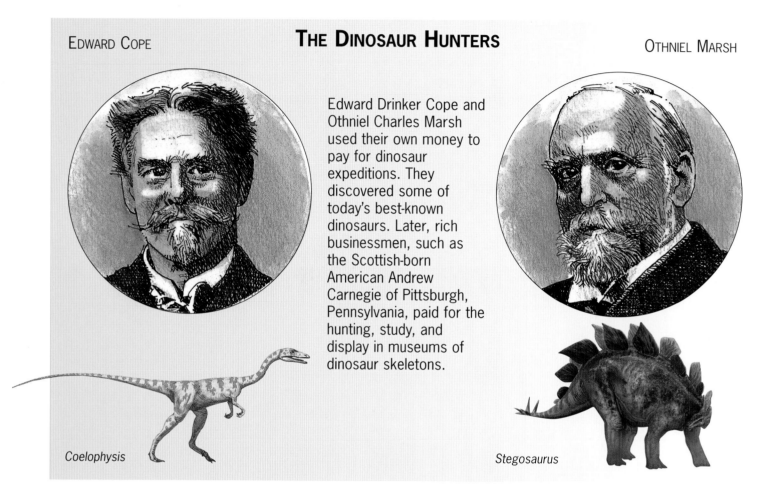

EDWARD COPE

THE DINOSAUR HUNTERS

OTHNIEL MARSH

Edward Drinker Cope and Othniel Charles Marsh used their own money to pay for dinosaur expeditions. They discovered some of today's best-known dinosaurs. Later, rich businessmen, such as the Scottish-born American Andrew Carnegie of Pittsburgh, Pennsylvania, paid for the hunting, study, and display in museums of dinosaur skeletons.

Coelophysis

Stegosaurus

While studies of *Iguanodon* were being carried out in Europe, the attention of many fossil hunters switched to North America, where many dinosaur finds were being made.

In 1877, a British fossil collector, Arthur Lakes, and a naval captain from Connecticut, H.C. Beckwith, found some big bones at the foot of the Rocky Mountains at Morrison, near Denver, Colorado. Lakes sent a message to Othniel Charles Marsh, who was professor of paleontology at Yale University, asking for help. Marsh was slow to reply, so Lakes sent a similar message to the wealthy scientist and fossil collector Edward Drinker Cope in Philadelphia, Pennsylvania.

This sparked what were to become known as the Bone Wars. Cope and Marsh did not like each other. When Marsh realized that his rival and a team of paleontologists were at Morrison, he sent out his own team to make new dinosaur discoveries. Both men realized that the layers of rocks here, which geologists call the Morrison Formation, were going to be rich in fossils. Both Cope and Marsh hired workers armed with pistols and rifles, and each poached the other's men and their fossil finds. It is said that one

team would take what they wanted from an area and smash up everything else so that the other team would not get it. Most of the fighting centered on a hill in Wyoming called Como Bluff. There, huge numbers of dinosaur fossils could be seen at the surface.

During the Bone Wars many dinosaur fossils may have been destroyed, but the wars did do some good. Both Cope and Marsh wanted to get their finds published and presented to science as quickly as possible, so they developed a way of uncovering the bones without damaging them. They left each bone partly buried in the rock and covered it with plaster of Paris. Then they cut out a block of rock with the bone still in it. The bone was removed from the rock in a laboratory, where it was easier to work. This technique is still used today. By the late 1890s, many new dinosaurs had been discovered. Marsh had found, among others, *Stegosaurus* and *Allosaurus*, while Cope had found *Camarasaurus* and *Coelophysis*.

▲ Dressed and armed for the dinosaur hunt, Marsh—center of back row—and his men pose for the camera.

▲ Arthur Lakes was not only a fossil hunter but also an artist. He painted this picture of Marsh's men at work at Como Bluff.

DIGGING UP THE PAST

Since the days of Cope and Marsh, the hunt for dinosaurs has spread to all the continents. In the early years of the last century, many discoveries were made in Canada, particularly in Alberta. Then Africa became the center for dinosaur discoveries. Between 1909 and 1929, in what is now Tanzania, German and British expeditions found dinosaurs like those of the Morrison Formation. In the 1920s, American expeditions to Mongolia found many fossil dinosaurs, including, for the first time, dinosaur eggs. Polish scientists, many of them women, worked in Mongolia from 1963 to 1971. Since the early 1990s, spectacular dinosaur discoveries have come from Mongolia, China, Argentina, and Africa, as well as the United States.

Today, paleontologists may set out to explore remote places where dinosaur bones are known to be common. The most important part of such trips is the preparation. A dinosaur-hunting expedition can cost tens of thousands of dollars. It may take many years to persuade governments and universities that they should pay for the trip. Politics may be a problem, too. Often the new

EXPOSED BY SCIENCE
Dinosaur skeletons are usually found by teams of scientists who know in what types and ages of rocks to look for them.

UNCOVERED IN DESERTS
Desert winds wear away the rock, and fossils of dinosaur footprints in rocks are exposed.

WASHED OUT BY RIVERS
A river wearing away a hillside will expose the fossils in the rock layers of a hill.

dinosaur sites are situated in developing countries where there are civil wars or conflicts between neighboring peoples, and some dinosaur-hunting expeditions need armed guards.

Once a dinosaur skeleton has been found, a team of expert fossil hunters moves in. The team tries to find out the species of dinosaur the skeleton came from and how best to remove it.

Unearthing the skeleton

The fossil hunters clear away the rocks above the bed containing the skeleton. When they have dug down close to the skeleton, the heavy earth-moving machines are taken away, and the rest of the rock above the fossils is cleared by hand. As each part of the skeleton is uncovered, it is drawn, measured, and photographed.

EXPOSED BY RAIN
Rain washes away soft clays, leaving hard fossils lying on the ground.

FOUND BY CHANCE
People walking along a riverbank or digging in a field may come across fossil bones.

If the skeleton is buried in solid rock, the whole rock bed is cut into large blocks, which are carried by truck to the museum. If the bones lie in soft material such as clay, however, the team clears away the clay above the bones by hand. The exposed bones are coated with wet paper and then with bandages or cloth soaked in plaster of Paris. The bone packages can then be carried off safely to the museum for the detailed work on the fossils.

Uncovering the bones

The paleontologists examine tiny fossils and structures in the rock and bones to build up a picture of the ancient landscape.

Back at the museum, technicians known as preparators carefully remove the protective plaster cases or the rock containing the bones. They use power tools, fine dental probes, and even pins and sewing needles. Sometimes the preparators use chemicals to dissolve the rock or sound waves to shake bones free. Finally, the bones are ready for the paleontologists to study.

THE BONES OF A DINOSAUR

If a dinosaur skeleton removed from rocks or the ground is almost complete, the museum may decide to put it on display instead of keeping it in the laboratory for study. (Only rarely are complete dinosaur skeletons found.)

The scientists must first know the structure of the animal when it was alive—how its bones were joined together, how the joints moved, and whether it stood on two or four legs.

Making a dinosaur display is like building a skyscraper. A steel framework is built to support the skeleton. If the bones are too delicate to handle, a copy of the skeleton is made and this is displayed instead. First, molds are made from the bones, and replicas are cast from them. The casts are arranged as a skeleton on the framework in a lifelike pose.

The casts have traditionally been made from plaster, as in Waterhouse Hawkins's original mount of *Hadrosaurus*. Today, lighter-weight materials, such as hollow fiberglass, are used. The Museum of Natural History in Denver, Colorado, has a 40-foot-long *Tyrannosaurus* skeleton that is so light it stands on one leg.

If a display dinosaur has any bones missing, casts of these are made from the bones of other skeletons of the same animal. Or sculptors make replicas based on what the paleontologists think the original bones may have looked like. Casts can be made many times from the molds, and so several museums may have mounted skeletons made from the same specimen.

SIDE TO SIDE, OR UP AND DOWN?
The tail of *Allosaurus* was tall and narrow. This suggests that it could move its tail from side to side more easily than it could move it up and down.

FLEXIBLE OR STIFF?
Some dinosaur tail bones were surrounded by very long bony bars, making the tail rigid. This is not the case in *Allosaurus*.

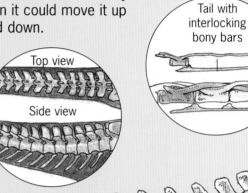

Top view

Side view

Tail with interlocking bony bars

▼ Articulated skeletons, such as this one of *Allosaurus*, are rare. When they are found, they are often used as the basis for a spectacular museum display.

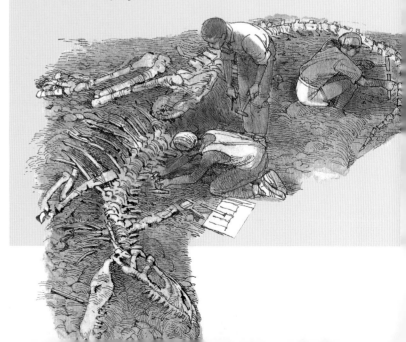

◀ Professor Peter Dodson, the scientific consultant for this book, examines some fossil bones on a dinosaur dig in Egypt.

SKELETON OF
ALLOSAURUS

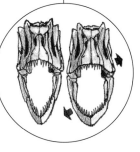

"OPEN WIDE"
The way the jawbones hang from the main part of the skull shows how the animals ate. Many meat eaters had jaws that expanded sideways, allowing them to swallow huge chunks of meat.

STRAIGHT OR BENT?
Allosaurus's knee joint shows that its hind legs were bent most of the time.

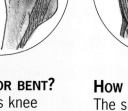

HOW BIG A CHEST?
The size of the chest cavity gives clues about the size of the internal organs.

FLESH ON THE BONES

• MUSCLES • ORGANS • SKIN •

The next step in the restoration is to put muscles on the bones. In life the muscles were attached by tendons, and these sometimes left marks where they were connected to the bones. The scientist needs to understand what forces the dinosaur would have needed to move the various parts of its body, and then the scientist can work out how the muscles would have been arranged to produce those forces.

With muscles over the bones, it is possible to get a good idea of the overall shape and size of the dinosaur. But for a complete restoration, the scientist also has to work out how parts of the body deep beneath the skin were laid out. This

requires an understanding of the habits and behavior of the dinosaur—its lifestyle. If it had been warm-blooded, it would have needed a great deal of energy. The heart and the lungs may have been large, like those of an elephant. The lungs may have had extra air sacs to take as much oxygen as possible from each breath, as do the lungs of modern birds. As a cold-blooded animal, it would have needed only small lungs, more like those of a crocodile.

The outer covering is the most speculative. For most dinosaurs we have no idea what their

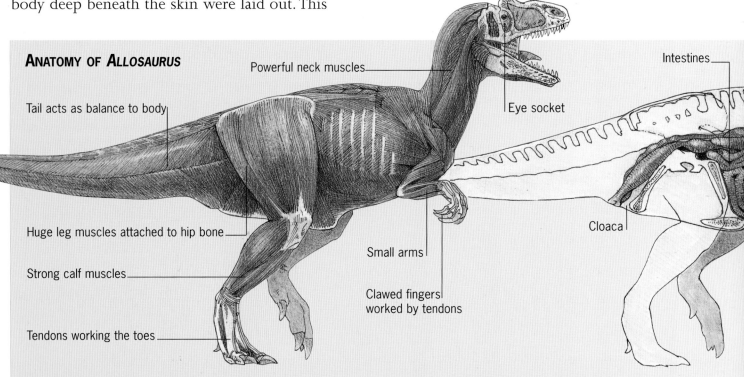

ANATOMY OF ALLOSAURUS

Powerful neck muscles

Intestines

Tail acts as balance to body

Eye socket

Huge leg muscles attached to hip bone

Cloaca

Strong calf muscles

Small arms

Clawed fingers worked by tendons

Tendons working the toes

MUSCLES

Leg muscles in an enormous two-footed animal such as this dinosaur must have been very large. The muscles that were needed to move its small forelimbs would have been less powerful. The

muscles attached to each bone of its tail would have been quite small. There are no fossils of dinosaur muscles, but paleontologists can estimate the size of muscle needed for each action or movement and build up the restoration from this information.

▲ The skin of a modern crocodile is made up of horny lumps and scales of different sizes. Scientists can only speculate that dinosaurs had similar body coverings.

skins were like. For a few, we have skin imprints, which are marks made as skin was pressed into soft ground.

Deciding on the skin color is more difficult. There is no evidence available. We believe that dinosaurs had good eyesight and could see colors, so we can be fairly sure that skin color played a part in their lives. Big showy bumps on the head and sail-like structures on the back were probably colorful for signaling. Dinosaurs that hunted may have had striped or spotted skins like tigers. Plant-eating animals may well have been camouflaged. Youngsters may have been striped or dappled. We can only make comparisons with the color schemes of modern animals. What helps today's creatures survive may also have worked for dinosaurs.

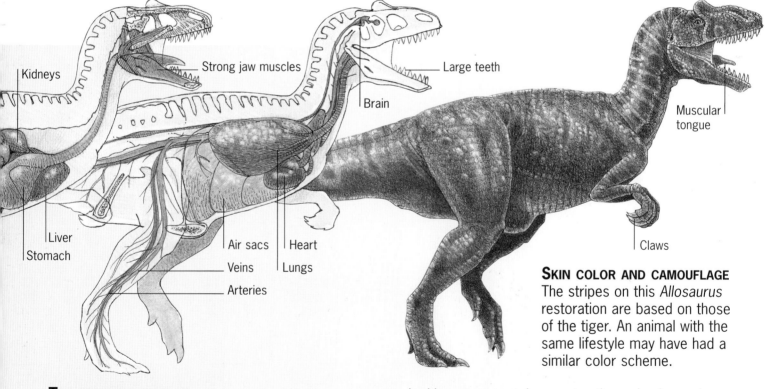

THE DIGESTIVE ORGANS

The guts—the stomach and intestines—of a meat-eating dinosaur would have been much smaller than the large complex guts needed to break down and get nutrients from plant food. We know this by

SKIN COLOR AND CAMOUFLAGE

The stripes on this *Allosaurus* restoration are based on those of the tiger. An animal with the same lifestyle may have had a similar color scheme.

looking at present-day meat-eating animals, such as cats and dogs, and plant-eating animals, such as cows and rabbits. Comparison with modern animals is an important part of restoring and reconstructing a dinosaur's body.

DINOSAUR FASCINATION

Even after the body of the dinosaur has been restored, the job of the paleontologist is only half done. The animal's lifestyle, its fellow creatures, and its surroundings must also be reconstructed in order to create a complete picture of the living beast. Detective work is used to finish the puzzle.

A famous example of a dinosaur puzzle rests in Wyoming. The fossil of a broken *Camarasaurus* skeleton—a long-necked plant eater—lies exposed on a shelf of sandstone and limestone rock. The softer rock, siltstone, that once covered the dinosaur has been worn away. Among the scattered bones are the broken teeth of the big meat-eating dinosaur *Ceratosaurus* and the small meat eater *Ornitholestes*. The *Camarasaurus* bones are scored with deep toothmarks, mostly the size of the teeth of *Allosaurus*, another meat eater.

From these details the paleontologists have worked out a possible story: The *Camarasaurus* lived on a dry plain, since the special mix of carbonate nodules and sandstone in the shelf is found only in this type of landscape. One *Camarasaurus* moved away from the main herd and was attacked and killed by an *Allosaurus*. Once the *Allosaurus* had eaten its meal, it moved off. The remains were set upon by a group of scavenging *Ceratosaurus*. What was left was finished off by the packs of *Ornitholestes* that had been waiting around like jackals while the bigger animals took the tastiest pieces. Not long afterward, a nearby river flooded, covering the plain and the skeleton with silt. This sediment gradually became the siltstone that lay on top of the fossils.

There are other explanations, but the fossil

▼ Reconstructions of dinosaur skeletons are put on display in museums. When we look at skeletons like these, we can create in our own minds pictures of ancient landscapes and living creatures.

▲ Modern museum reconstructions and restorations, such as this one at the Natural History Museum, London, try to show not only the animal but also its surroundings and its lifestyle. They try to present the known facts as a completed jigsaw-puzzle picture.

site shows interaction between the dinosaurs that lived there long ago.

Why do we find dinosaurs so fascinating and fun? It is probably for the same reasons that we like stories of monsters and dragons. We have a natural interest in things that are bizarre and frightening. We enjoy imagining what they were or could be like.

Ever since the dinosaurs' fossilized bones were recognized for what they are and the name dinosaur was created, more than 160 years ago, the idea of extinct monsters has gripped people's imaginations and interest. Younger children can pronounce the creatures' names before they can read and write. Dinosaur displays are among the most popular parts of museums. Dinosaurs appear in comic strips, as toys, as badges, as advertising logos, in the forms of cookies, and on postage stamps.

Dinosaurs have always been popular in the works of literature, from Jules Verne's *Journey to the Center of the Earth* to modern science fiction novels, such as Michael Crichton's *Jurassic Park*. These works have also made exciting movies. The spectacular images produced on movie screens lend themselves well to visions of fantastic creatures. The first *King Kong*, made in 1933, was the dinosaur classic of the first talking motion pictures. Television spectaculars such as *Walking with Dinosaurs* presented dinosaurs in a more factual documentary manner. The moviemakers used models, costumed actors, lizards fitted with horns and sails, and images created completely on computers to give us a glimpse of a prehistoric world.

DO YOU KNOW?

When did the dinosaurs first appear?
The earliest dinosaurs we currently know are
Herrerasaurus, *Staurikosaurus*, and *Eoraptor*. These meat
eaters lived at the start of the Late Triassic Period
in South America. They evolved from the
crocodile-like thecodonts about 225 million
years ago.

When did the dinosaurs die out?
Dinosaurs became extinct at the very end of the
Cretaceous Period, about 65 million years ago.
For a few million years before then, the
numbers of dinosaurs had been getting smaller.
But suddenly all these animals, and many others,
died out.

How are dinosaurs named?
A dinosaur's proper scientific name (in fact, the
proper scientific name for all animals) consists
of two parts. The first part, the genus name, has
a capital letter. The second part, the species
name, does not. Both names are written in
italics but only the genus name is capitalized.
Very similar species or kinds of dinosaurs are
grouped together in the same genus. That is why
we sometimes use the whole name, such as
Tyrannosaurus rex. More often, we just use the
genus name, such as *Tyrannosaurus*.

How many kinds of dinosaurs were there?
Scientists know of more than 500 different
dinosaur genera (*genera* is the plural of *genus*).
This probably represents about 30 percent of
all dinosaur genera that existed.

Which were the most southerly dinosaurs?
We used to say that dinosaurs have been found
on all the continents except Antarctica. The early
1990s changed all that. Expeditions to several
sites in Antarctica uncovered all kinds of
dinosaur remains, including a big meat eater
with a curly crest, called *Cryolophosaurus*, and
others related to *Dilophosaurus* and to *Coelophysis*, as
well as many kinds of plant eaters related to
Hypsilophodon and an ankylosaur, *Antarctopelta*.
Antarctica must have had a much milder climate
in Jurassic times.

Which were the most northerly dinosaurs?
Remains of duckbilled dinosaurs and horned
dinosaurs, as well as the teeth of *Troodon*-like
animals, have been found in Late Cretaceous
rocks in Alaska. In Late Cretaceous times this
area would have been hundreds of miles farther
north than it is today. Footprints like those of
Iguanodon have been found in Early Cretaceous
rocks of the Arctic Islands of Spitsbergen.

Which was the tallest dinosaur?
Sauroposeidon, a long-necked plant eater like
Brachiosaurus, could have raised its head to a
height of 55 feet above the ground.

Which was the heaviest dinosaur?
As far as we know, *Argentinosaurus* was the heaviest
as well as one of the tallest. In life it would have
weighed 100 tons. However, part of a bone
belonging to a *Brachiosaurus*-like dinosaur was
found in 1987, and this could be from an
animal weighing about 130 tons.

Which was the longest dinosaur?
Seismosaurus, or "earthquake reptile," was a long-
necked plant eater like *Diplodocus*. From the

incomplete skeleton discovered in 1985, scientists think the whole animal must have been more than 130 feet long.

Which dinosaur had the biggest skull?

The ceratopsians—the horned dinosaurs—with their big frills covering their necks, had the biggest skulls. *Torosaurus* and *Pentaceratops* had frilled skulls that were 9 feet long—the longest skulls known of any land animal ever.

Which dinosaur had the biggest eyes?

Dromiceiomimus had eyes that were about 3 inches in diameter.

Which dinosaur had the biggest teeth?

The biggest meat-eating teeth known are from *Giganotosaurus*, which are about a foot long, including the roots. The biggest plant-eating teeth known are from *Iguanodon*-like *Lanzhousaurus* and are over 8 inches long with the roots.

Which dinosaur had the longest neck?

A complete skeleton of *Mamenchisaurus*, a *Diplodocus*-like long-necked plant eater from China, has a neck that is 36 feet long, the longest known of any animal.

Which dinosaur had the longest horns?

The three-horned dinosaur *Triceratops* had a horn on its nose and one over each eye. The bony cores of the eye horns were more than 3 feet long. They must have been much longer in life, when they were covered with horny sheaths.

Which was the smallest dinosaur?

Microraptor was the smallest, about 16 inches long. The little meat eater *Compsognathus*, with a length of 3 feet and a weight of 5 pounds, used to be thought of as the smallest dinosaur. Remains of a shorter but heavier dinosaur found in Colorado were from a two-footed plant eater

related to *Scutellosaurus* but without the armor. It probably weighed about 15 pounds but was only about 2½ feet long.

Which was the smallest horned dinosaur?

This was *Graciliceratops*—"graceful horned face"—from Late Cretaceous China. This dinosaur was about 30 inches long and was built like *Hypsilophodon*, but it had a neck frill.

Which is the smallest baby dinosaur known?

Nests of *Troodon* lie in rocks in Montana. One of the eggs contains an embryo that is 4 inches long. The 8-inch-long skeleton of a young *Mussaurus* has been found, but its tail is missing.

Did any dinosaurs climb trees?

Scientists used to believe that *Hypsilophodon* climbed trees. This was because it was built like the modern tree kangaroo and because the foot bones seemed to have been adapted to perching. We know now that this was not the case. *Hypsilophodon* was a sprinter. A small birdlike dinosaur, *Microraptor*, from China, probably climbed trees and glided from the branches.

Which was the smallest armored dinosaur?

Struthiosaurus from Late Cretaceous eastern Europe was only about 6 feet long.

What was the smallest tyrannosaur?

Dilong from the Early Cretaceous of China was only 5 feet long.

What is the longest dinosaur name?

So far, *Micropachycephalosaurus*, meaning "little thick-head reptile," with 23 letters, has the longest dinosaur name. It is also one of the smallest dinosaurs. This dome-headed, two-footed plant eater was about 20 inches long. Among the shortest dinosaur names is *Minmi* with 5 letters, named after the site in Australia where it was found. Also with five letters is *Khaan*, from Mongolia, an oviraptorid. But the shortest of all is *Mei* from China.

Which dinosaur had the smallest brain in relation to its body size?

Stegosaurus had a brain that weighed 2 or 3 ounces and was the size of three Ping-Pong balls. This was only 1/250,000 the weight of its body. (Our brains are about 1/50 of our weight.)

Which were the most intelligent dinosaurs?

The meat eaters, particularly small meat eaters such as *Troodon*, had the biggest brains in relation to their size. Most of the brain capacity, however, was used for sight, hearing, and other skills needed for hunting, and they would have only been about as brainy as modern opossums.

What was the first mounted dinosaur skeleton?

The skeleton of *Hadrosaurus* was the first ever on display. It was largely made-up plaster-model bones built around the original fossils, and it was mounted by Waterhouse Hawkins under Joseph Leidy's direction in the Academy of Natural Sciences in Philadelphia in 1868.

What is the biggest mounted dinosaur skeleton?

The skeleton of *Brachiosaurus* in the Humboldt Museum in Berlin is 72 feet long. It stands 19 feet, 8 inches high at the shoulders, and the head is 39 feet above the ground.

What is the tallest mounted dinosaur skeleton?

A skeleton of *Barosaurus*, a long-necked plant eater like *Diplodocus*, stands in the American Museum of Natural History in New York City. The skeleton is shown rearing up on its hind legs, and its head is 55 feet high.

What is the biggest known dinosaur bone?

The biggest bone is the solid hip structure of a long-necked plant eater found in Colorado in 1988, close to where the remains of *Supersaurus* were discovered in the late 1970s. This structure, consisting of the hip bones and the vertebrae (backbones) attached to it, measures 6 feet high and 4 feet, 6 inches long, and weighs 1,500 pounds. The longest single bone of any dinosaur, probably of any vertebrate, is a neck rib of the sauropod *Mamenchisaurus* from northwestern China. It measures 13 feet, 5 inches.

Did any dinosaurs survive beyond the Cretaceous Period?

Now and again fossil dinosaur-like teeth are found in rocks that date from after the end of the Cretaceous Period 65 million years ago. Some of the teeth belonged to a kind of land-living crocodile and not to a dinosaur at all. Others are yet unidentified. A number of scientists say that birds evolved from dinosaurs, so although dinosaurs are extinct, their descendants are all around us today!

What was the first dinosaur movie?

The first dinosaur movie was a silent cartoon film called *Gertie the Dinosaur*, made by Windsor McCay in 1912. Gertie was, in fact, the first character ever to be designed for a cartoon. The first animated model dinosaur was an *Apatosaurus* filmed in 1914 by Willis O'Brien, who later animated the dinosaurs for *The Lost World* made in 1925 and the first *King Kong* in 1933.

Which was the fastest dinosaur?

A little dinosaur living in Arizona in the Early Jurassic Period left intriguing footprints in the rocks. The animal weighed about 20 pounds and yet made footprints that were about 12 feet apart. Scientists have worked out that the animal must have been running at 40 miles an hour.

alga a very primitive type of plant, such as a seaweed.

ammonite one of an ancient group of shelled animals, related to modern squid, cuttlefish, and octopuses. Ammonites died out at the same time as the dinosaurs.

amphibian a four-legged vertebrate animal (one with a backbone) that lays its eggs in water but usually spends its adult stage on land. Examples of modern amphibians include frogs, salamanders, and newts.

anatomy the study of the structure of living things—for example, how a dinosaur's bones fitted together, and the size and shape of the various parts.

atmosphere the layer of gases that surrounds Earth; also known as the air.

beak a horny mouth structure that occurs on birds and some dinosaurs. It is more lightweight than a set of teeth but is used in much the same way.

Labyrinthodont, a 10-foot long amphibian of dinosaur times.

browse to feed on shoots, leaves, and bark of shrubs and trees.

camouflage a natural color scheme or pattern that allows an animal to blend in with its surroundings so that it will not be noticed.

carnivore a meat-eating animal.

cast the shape that results when the space inside a mold is filled with a fluid substance that later becomes solid.

cheek pouch a fold of skin and muscle at the side of the mouth that holds food during chewing.

climate the average weather conditions in a particular part of the world.

coal a rock made from the remains of ancient plants that were buried and squashed by mud, silt, and sand being laid on top of them.

cold-blooded term used to describe an animal that cannot control the temperature of its body except by moving between warm and cool environments—for example, a fish.

colonization the way in which a new type of plant or animal gradually takes over a new living area.

conifer tree a tree that produces seeds in cones—for example, a pine, fir, or larch. Its needlelike leaves usually stay on the tree all year.

continent one of the huge areas of land, or landmasses, on Earth. They are always slowly moving and changing. The continents of today are, in descending order of size, Asia, Africa, North America, South America, Antarctica, Europe, and Australia.

core the innermost part of Earth, probably made of iron. The inner core is probably solid and the outer core is liquid.

crest a structure on top of the head, usually for display.

Classopolis conifer

Cretaceous the period of geological time between 145 and 65 million years ago. It was the final period of the Age of Dinosaurs that led up to the end of the dinosaurs.

crust the rocky outer skin of Earth, lying on the mantle.

cycad a plant related to the conifers, consisting of a stout trunk and a bunch of palmlike leaves.

cycadeoid an ancient plant with a swollen trunk that resembled the modern cycads.

deposit in geology, rock material such as sand and pebbles laid down in an area after having been carried from elsewhere by rivers, wind, glaciers, or the sea.

digest to break down food in the stomach and intestines into a form that can be absorbed and used by the body.

environment the total of the living conditions of an animal, including the landscape, the climate, the plants growing in the area, and all the other animals that live all around.

evolve to change, over many generations, to produce a new species.

fang a long, pointed tooth.

fern a nonflowering plant with broad, finely divided leaves known as fronds.

fiberglass glass in the form of very fine strands. When mixed with gluelike substances, it forms a tough and lightweight material.

flash flood a sudden rush of water down a river valley after rainfall in nearby mountains.

fossil a part or trace of a once-living plant or animal that is preserved in rocks.

fossilized turned into fossils.

frond a finely divided leaf such as one found on a fern or palm tree.

geology the study of Earth—the rocks and minerals that compose it, the history of its formation, and the fossils of the animals that once lived here.

ginkgo a coniferous tree that sheds broad heart-shaped leaves in the fall. There is only one living species, the Maidenhair tree.

Gondwana the southern section of the ancient continent of Pangaea, consisting of what is now South America, Africa, India, Australia, and Antarctica.

Fern

graze to eat low-growing plants. Modern grazers eat grass and include sheep, goats, many antelope, and cattle.

greenhouse effect a heating up of Earth's surface because a change in the makeup of the atmosphere stops the warmth from the ground from escaping into space.

growth ring a ring of bone or wood produced as an animal or a tree grows. Animals and plants may grow at different speeds at various times of the year, and this is seen as layers of light and dark colors in a cross-section of the bone or wood.

hatchling an animal that is newly hatched from its egg.

herbivore a plant-eating animal.

hoof (pl. hooves) a very tough and heavy toenail built to take the weight of an animal.

horn a tough, shiny substance made of the same chemical material as hair, and often formed as a protective covering on some part of an animal. The name is also used for a pointed structure covered with horn.

horsetail plant a plant, related to the fern, with sprays of green branches along an upright stem and tiny leaves.

ichthyosaur a swimming reptile of Triassic, Jurassic, and Cretaceous times that was so adapted to life in the water that it looked like a modern-day dolphin.

impression a mark or print in the surface of the ground or a rock made by something pressing against or in it.

intestine the part of the food canal beyond the stomach from which the nutrients are absorbed into the blood for use by the cells and tissues of the body.

Jurassic the period of geological time between 200 and 145 million years ago. It is the middle period of the Age of Dinosaurs.

Laurasia the northern section of Pangaea, consisting of what is now North America, Europe, and most of Asia.

life-span the length of time an animal lives.

limestone a rock made up mainly of the mineral calcite. Some limestones are formed from the calcite of shells of sea animals that died long ago and were buried on the sea bed. Freshwater limestones may form in lakes.

lung fish a fish that has lungs as well as gills, so it can breathe air. Lung fish can survive droughts or live in stagnant waters.

mammal a vertebrate (backboned) animal that produces live young and feeds them on milk. Modern mammals include cats, dogs, mice, rabbits, whales, monkeys, ourselves, and many other species.

mammal-like reptile a member of a group of reptiles that were common in the Permian Period, before dinosaurs evolved. These reptiles developed a variety of mammal-like features such as teeth of different sizes. They eventually evolved into the mammals themselves.

mantle the stony layer that makes up the bulk of Earth. It is solid, but with a soft layer near the top.

meteorite a lump of rock from space that falls to Earth.

migrate to move from place to place as conditions change to find new sources of food or shelter, or to mate and bring up young.

mineral a substance that is formed naturally in the ground. All rocks are made of minerals, which include mixtures of elements such as iron, aluminum, potassium, carbon, silicon, oxygen, and hydrogen.

mold a hollow container, having the shape of a particular object, into which a liquid is poured. When the liquid hardens, it takes the object's shape. The copy of the object is known as a cast.

molecule the smallest particle of a chemical compound formed by the joining together of atoms, the building units of all matter.

Ornithischia the bird-hipped dinosaurs, including the two-footed plant eaters, the plated dinosaurs, the armored dinosaurs, the dome-headed dinosaurs and the horned dinosaurs.

ornithopod a two-footed plant-eating dinosaur, such as *Iguanodon*.

paleontologist a person who studies paleontology, the science of living things of earlier times as known from the examination of fossils.

Pangaea the name given to the supercontinent that once existed in which all the continental masses of Earth were joined together.

Permian the period of geological time between 299 and 251 million years ago; the time when the reptiles were taking over from the amphibians and the period immediately before dinosaurs appeared.

plaster of Paris a mixture of fine powder that sets hard when mixed with water. It is used to make casts in pottery or to protect a person's broken bones until they have healed.

plesiosaur a swimming reptile from the Age of Dinosaurs that had a squat body, paddles as limbs, and either a long neck and small head or a short neck and big head.

predator a meat-eating animal that hunts and kills other animals for food.

Rat-size *Megazostrodon* is one of the earliest-known mammals.

prehistoric in ancient times; before written historical records.

prey an animal that is hunted and eaten by a predator.

pterosaur a member of a group of flying reptiles, related to the dinosaurs, that flew using wings of skin and lived during the Triassic, Jurassic, and Cretaceous periods.

quicksand a dangerous area of wet sand that may become almost liquid when stepped on.

reconstruction the skeleton of an animal rebuilt from its bones or casts of the bones.

reptile cold-blooded vertebrate (backboned) animal that lays hard-shelled or leathery eggs on land. Snakes, lizards, turtles, terrapins, and crocodiles are modern types of reptiles. Dinosaurs have always been regarded as reptiles, even though it is now accepted that at least some of them were warm-blooded.

restoration a picture or a model of an animal as it appeared in life. This may include showing the surroundings of the animal.

sandstone a rock formed from sand particles cemented together.

Saurischia the lizard-hipped dinosaurs, including the meat eaters and the long-necked plant eaters.

sauropod a long-necked plant-eating dinosaur, such as *Apatosaurus*.

scale in reptiles, a small leaf of horn that forms part of the outer covering.

scavenger a meat-eating animal that does not make its own kills but eats the bodies of animals that are already dead.

sediment tiny pieces of soil, earth, or rock—for example, grains of sand or specks of mud—that are deposited at the bottom of the sea or on a river bed.

silt a sediment that is finer than sand but coarser than mud.

siltstone rock formed from silt particles cemented together by pressure from layers of more sediment from above.

species a collection of animals, or any living things, in which individuals look like one another and share a common ancestry. In higher animals, individuals of the same species can breed with one another to produce young. Breeding, reproduction, and mating are all terms to describe the process by which individuals make more of their species.

tendon a tough piece of animal tissue that attaches the muscle to the bone.

theropod a meat-eating dinosaur, such as *Tyrannosaurus*.

tree fern a plant of the fern group that grows to 80 feet or more in height. There are only a few living species now, but they were plentiful at the beginning of the Age of Dinosaurs.

Triassic the period of geological time between 251 and 200 million years ago. The dinosaurs first appeared in the Triassic Period.

vertebrate an animal that has a backbone. Vertebrates include the fish, amphibians, reptiles, birds, and mammals. As mammals, we are also vertebrates.

vocal cords the structures in the throat of many vertebrates that vibrate and produce a noise as air passes over them.

voice box the structure in the throat of an animal in which the voice is produced. This usually contains the vocal cords.

warm-blooded term used to describe an animal that can regulate its own body temperature—for example, a mammal or a bird.

Rhamphorhynchus pterosaur

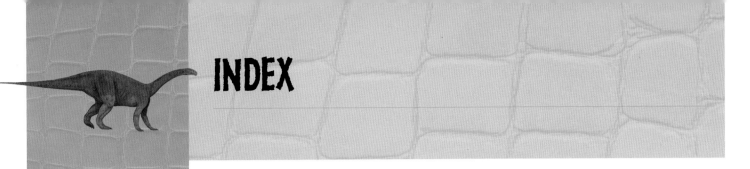

INDEX

ACKNOWLEDGMENTS

PHOTO CREDITS
Corbis Inc.: pages 38, 57, 99, 116; Digital Vision: pages 31, 43, 47, 67, 69, 78, 94, 109, 113, 119, 127, 147; Peter Dodson: page 145; Eyewire: pages 40, 101, 115; iStockphotos: pages 65 (Jurie Maree), 73 (Nancy Nehring), 81 (Valerie Crafter), 83 (Jennifer Sheets), 89 (Robert Appelbaum), 93 (Paul Wolf), 97 (Eline Spek), 123 (Markanja), 126 (Joe McDaniel), 129 (Valérie Koch), 133 (Duard van der Westhuizen), 148 (Beth Skwarecki); Natural History Museum Photo Library, London: page 149 (John Downs); Yale Peabody Museum of Natural History: page 141, both images.

ARTIST CREDITS
James Field, Chris Forsey, James Robins, Steve Kirk, Denys Ovenden.

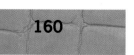